MW01489088

YELLOWSTONE

NATIONAL PARK
TRAVEL GUIDE
2025

YELLOWSTONE NATIONAL PARK TRAVEL GUIDE 2025

A New Pocket Manual for Exploring Hidden Gems, Spotting Wildlife, Camping Tips, and Must-See Geysers for an Unforgettable Adventure

Michael D. Nelson

TABLE OF CONTENTS

TABLE OF CONTENTS

TABLE OF CONTENTS

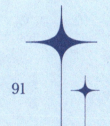

TABLE OF CONTENTS

COPYRIGHT

All rights reserved. Before this document is duplicated or reproduced in any manner, the publisher's consent must be gained. Therefore, the contents within can neither be stored electronically, transferred, nor kept in a database. Neither in Part nor full can the document be copied, scanned, faxed, or retained without approval from the publisher or creator.

Copyright © Michael D. Nelson 2025

MAP OF YELLOWSTONE NATIONAL PARK

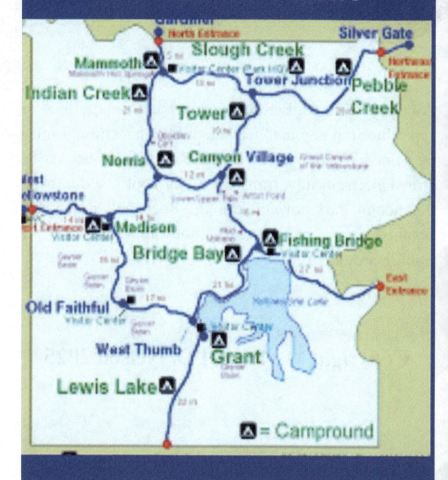

INTRODUCTION

Imagine driving with the windows down, the smell of pine trees filling the air, and suddenly you see steam rising from the ground. You've arrived at Yellowstone National Park! Leave your worries behind. Yellowstone is a place where you can escape the everyday and reconnect with nature. It's a place where you can witness incredible geothermal features, diverse wildlife, and breathtaking landscapes.

This is more than just a national park; it's a living, breathing ecosystem. You can see bison roaming free, watch a geyser erupt high into the sky, and hike through forests and mountains. You might even spot a wolf or a grizzly bear! Yellowstone is a one-of-a-kind adventure.

With this guide, you'll discover the best places to visit, where to stay, and how to make the most of your trip. We'll share insider tips on planning your itinerary, choosing the right accommodations, and staying safe while exploring the park's wild side.

CHAPTER 1: PLANNING YOUR YELLOWSTONE EXPEDITION

Best Time to Visit Yellowstone

Keep in mind that many park services, like lodging and restaurants, begin to close by mid-September, so plan ahead. But if you're seeking a quieter, more serene Yellowstone experience, fall is the perfect time.

Winter (November to March)

Yellowstone in winter is like stepping into a snow globe. The park takes on a stillness that's almost otherworldly. The geothermal features—geysers, hot springs, and fumaroles—create a mesmerizing mist in the cold air. With temperatures ranging from 10°F to 30°F, winter is ideal for those seeking solitude, snowshoeing, cross-country skiing, and even snowmobiling. It's also an excellent time to spot wolves in the Lamar Valley. Be prepared for the cold and know that only certain areas of the park are accessible during this season. Winter travel requires planning and flexibility, but the rewards are unmatched for those seeking a true escape.

There's truly no wrong time to experience the magic of Yellowstone, but when you visit can greatly shape your adventure. Whether you're hoping to avoid crowds, catch the best wildlife sightings, or witness the park draped in its seasonal glory, timing is key. Let's break down the best times to visit based on the kind of experience you're seeking.

Summer (June to August)

Summer is Yellowstone's most popular season, and for good reason. With temperatures ranging from the mid-60s to low 80s (°F), it's perfect for outdoor activities like hiking, wildlife viewing, and exploring the park's major attractions. All roads and facilities are fully open, and the park is bustling with life. This is the time for those iconic geyser shows and epic sunsets over the Grand Canyon of the Yellowstone. However, be prepared for crowds, especially around popular spots like Old Faithful and the Grand Prismatic Spring. If you don't mind the busy atmosphere, this is when the park is at its most accessible.

Fall (September to October)

Fall offers something truly special in Yellowstone: the beauty of changing leaves paired with cooler, crisper air. The crowds begin to thin, allowing you to savor the park at a more relaxed pace. Wildlife is abundant during this time, as elk enter their rutting season, bugling their haunting calls across the valleys. It's a photographer's dream, with snow-dusted peaks, vibrant foliage, and the soft golden light of autumn.

Spring (April to May)

Spring in Yellowstone is a time of renewal. The snow melts, and wildlife emerges from winter slumber. Temperatures can be unpredictable, ranging from chilly mornings to warmer afternoons. While some park areas may still be closed due to snow, it's a magical time to witness newborn animals, like bison calves and bear cubs, roaming the meadows. Spring offers smaller crowds and more peaceful moments in nature. Remember to pack layers, as the weather can change quickly, and some roads or trails may be impassable early in the season.

Getting There

Reaching Yellowstone National Park is the first step in your grand adventure. While flying is the most common way to get to Yellowstone, there are other options, such as driving, joining a bus tour, or taking a train. However, for those with limited time or who prefer a quicker arrival, flying is often the most convenient choice.

Yellowstone is accessible via several airports, each with its own set of advantages and considerations. Choosing the right airport can depend on factors like your budget, your origin city, and which part of the park you want to explore first. Let's take a closer look at each airport to help you make the best decision for your trip.

Jackson Hole Airport (JAC)

- Address: Jackson Hole Airport, 1250 E Airport Rd, Jackson, WY 83001
- Distance to Yellowstone: 57 miles to the South Entrance
- Average Cost of Flight: $250–$500 (depending on the season and departure city)

Located just 57 miles from the South Entrance, Jackson Hole Airport is the closest airport to Yellowstone. This makes it a convenient option for those who want to minimize travel time and get to the park quickly. Flying into Jackson Hole is also a scenic experience in itself, as the airport is nestled within Grand Teton National Park, offering stunning mountain views upon arrival. It's served by major airlines like Delta, United, and American Airlines, with modern amenities and typically short wait times. However, keep in mind that Jackson Hole is a smaller airport with potentially higher fares, especially during peak season.

Bozeman Yellowstone International Airport (BZN)

- Address: Bozeman Yellowstone International Airport, 850 Gallatin Field Rd, Bozeman, MT 59718
- Distance to Yellowstone: 90 miles to the North Entrance
- Average Cost of Flight: $200–$450 (depending on the season and departure city)

If you're looking for a good balance of convenience and affordability, Bozeman Yellowstone International Airport is a great option. Located about 90 miles from the North Entrance, Bozeman is well-connected to major cities with flights from Denver, Salt Lake City, Seattle, and more. It's a particularly good choice if you plan to explore the northern part of Yellowstone, including Mammoth Hot Springs and the wildlife-rich Lamar Valley. While generally more affordable than Jackson Hole, it's still recommended to book your flights early, especially if traveling during peak season.

Yellowstone Airport (WYS)

- Address: Yellowstone Airport, 50 N Electric St, West Yellowstone, MT 59758
- Distance to Yellowstone: 5 miles to the West Entrance
- Average Cost of Flight: $300–$500 (seasonal flights)

For the quickest possible entry into Yellowstone, consider Yellowstone Airport. Located just 5 miles from the West Entrance, this airport allows you to start your park adventure almost immediately. It's ideal for those who want to prioritize exploring the western side of Yellowstone, including Old Faithful, the Grand Prismatic Spring, and the Upper Geyser Basin.

However, it's important to note that Yellowstone Airport is a seasonal airport, operating mainly from June to September, with limited flight options and potentially higher prices.

Billings Logan International Airport (BIL)

- Address: Billings Logan International Airport, 1901 Terminal Cir, Billings, MT 59105
- Distance to Yellowstone: 130 miles to the Northeast Entrance
- Average Cost of Flight: $200–$400 (depending on the season)

If affordability is your top priority, Billings Logan International Airport is worth considering. Located about 130 miles from the Northeast Entrance, Billings offers a wider range of airlines and flights compared to other airports serving Yellowstone. This can often translate to cheaper fares and more flexibility in your travel plans. The drive from Billings to Yellowstone is also quite scenic, allowing you to enjoy the journey as part of your overall experience.

Salt Lake City International Airport (SLC)

- Address: Salt Lake City International Airport, 776 N Terminal Dr, Salt Lake City, UT 84122
- Distance to Yellowstone: 320 miles to the South Entrance
- Average Cost of Flight: $150–$350 (depending on the departure city)

While it's the farthest from Yellowstone at 320 miles to the south, Salt Lake City International Airport is a major hub with extensive flight options, including both domestic and international connections. This makes it a good choice for travelers who want to combine their Yellowstone trip with visits to other destinations in the region. Salt Lake City often has the most competitive fares, and the drive to Yellowstone offers opportunities to explore other national parks and scenic byways along the way.

Important Notes:

No matter which airport you choose, remember to book your flights and any rental cars well in advance, especially if you're traveling during peak season (June-August). Transportation from the airport to the park can be done by rental car, shuttle, or pre-arranged transportation through your lodging. Always check the respective airport websites for the most up-to-date flight information, schedules, and services.

BILLINGS LOGAN INTERNATIONAL AIRPORT

SCAN THE QR CODE

- Open your device's camera app
- Point the camera at the QR code
- Ensure the QR code is within the frame and well-lit
- Wait for your device to recognize the QR code
- Once recognized, tap on the map and input for current location for direction and distance to the destination

YELLOWSTONE AIRPORT

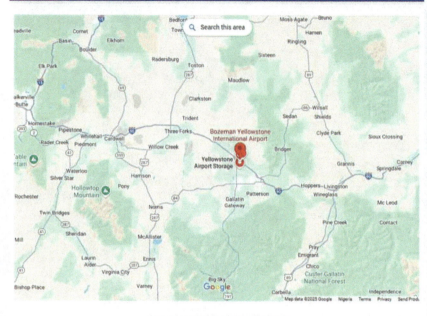

SCAN THE QR CODE

- Open your device's camera app
- Point the camera at the QR code
- Ensure the QR code is within the frame and well-lit
- Wait for your device to recognize the QR code
- Once recognized, tap on the map and input for current location for direction and distance to the destination

BOZEMAN YELLOWSTONE INTERNATIONAL AIRPORT

SCAN THE QR CODE

- Open your device's camera app
- Point the camera at the QR code
- Ensure the QR code is within the frame and well-lit
- Wait for your device to recognize the QR code
- Once recognized, tap on the map and input for current location for direction and distance to the destination

JACKSON HOLE AIRPORT (JAC)

SCAN THE QR CODE

- Open your device's camera app
- Point the camera at the QR code
- Ensure the QR code is within the frame and well-lit
- Wait for your device to recognize the QR code
- Once recognized, tap on the map and input for current location for direction and distance to the destination

Choosing the Best Accommodation

After a day of exploring Yellowstone's wonders, you'll want a cozy and comfortable place to rest and recharge. Luckily, the park and its surrounding areas offer a variety of lodging options to suit every taste and budget. Whether you dream of waking up to the sight of steaming geysers or prefer the rustic charm of a cabin nestled in the woods, Yellowstone has something for everyone.

In-Park Lodging

For those who want to be in the heart of the action, staying within the park is the way to go. Yellowstone boasts a collection of historic lodges and cabins, each with its own unique character and charm.

Old Faithful Inn

- Address: Old Faithful Inn, Yellowstone National Park, WY 82190
- Cost: Rates for rooms start at around $250–$400 per night, depending on the season.

Why Choose Old Faithful Inn:
- Iconic Historic Lodge: Experience the grandeur of one of the oldest and most famous lodges in the park, built in 1904.

- Prime Location: Steps away from the legendary Old Faithful Geyser.
- Rustic Charm: Enjoy the unique atmosphere and historic architecture.

Lake Yellowstone Hotel

- Address: Lake Yellowstone Hotel, Yellowstone National Park, WY 82190
- Cost: Rates range from $200–$500 per night.

Why Choose Lake Yellowstone Hotel:
- Elegant Lakeside Retreat: Relax in a historic hotel with exceptional service and stunning views of Yellowstone Lake.
- Refined Ambiance: Experience a touch of luxury in the heart of the wilderness.
- Perfect for Water Activities: Enjoy easy access to boating, fishing, and lakeside trails.

Mammoth Hot Springs Hotel

- Address: Mammoth Hot Springs Hotel, Yellowstone National Park, WY 82190
- Cost: Rates start at $150–$300 per night.

Why Choose Mammoth Hot Springs Hotel:
- Northern Gateway: Located near the park's North Entrance, ideal for exploring Mammoth Hot Springs terraces and the wildlife-rich Lamar Valley.
- Variety of Accommodations: Choose from historic rooms in the main building or modern cabins.

Campgrounds

For a true Yellowstone experience, pitch a tent or park your RV under the stars. The park offers a variety of campgrounds, from those with basic amenities to more remote sites for a secluded getaway.

Madison Campground

- Address: Madison Campground, Yellowstone National Park, WY 82190
- Cost: $20 per night for a standard campsite.

Why Choose Madison Campground:
- Popular and Convenient: Located near the West Entrance, offering easy access to geyser basins and the town of West Yellowstone.
- Amenities: Equipped with flush toilets, potable water, and picnic tables.

Slough Creek Campground

- Address: Slough Creek Campground, Yellowstone National Park, WY 82190
- Cost: $20 per night.

Why Choose Slough Creek Campground:
- Remote and Rustic: Located in the park's northeast corner, offering a secluded camping experience near Lamar Valley.
- Wildlife Viewing: Excellent opportunities to spot wolves, bison, and bears.

Nearby Hotels

If you prefer more flexibility or a wider range of amenities, consider staying in one of the towns bordering Yellowstone.

West Yellowstone, Montana

- Cost: Rates range from $100–$250 per night, depending on the type of accommodation.

Why Choose West Yellowstone:
- Gateway Town: Located just outside the park's West Entrance, offering a variety of hotels, motels, and vacation rentals.
- Amenities: Enjoy restaurants, shops, and other services.

Gardiner, Montana

- Cost: Rates range from $90–$250 per night.

Why Choose Gardiner:
- North Entrance Access: A charming town with budget-friendly options near the park's North Entrance.
- Scenic Setting: Located near the Yellowstone River, offering a peaceful atmosphere.

Tips for Choosing the Right Accommodation

- Book in Advance: Lodging within the park fills up quickly, especially during peak season. Make your reservations early!
- Consider Your Interests: Choose lodging near the attractions and activities you want to prioritize.
- Balance Your Budget: In-park lodging tends to be pricier, while nearby towns offer more budget-friendly options.
- Read Reviews: See what other travelers have to say about their experiences at different accommodations.

With careful planning, you'll find the perfect place to call home during your Yellowstone adventure.

Navigating the Park

Once you've arrived in Yellowstone, getting around this vast and diverse park is an adventure in itself. Covering over 2.2 million acres, Yellowstone requires a bit of planning to ensure you can see and do all the things you desire. Whether you prefer the freedom of driving your own car, the convenience of shuttle services, or the immersive experience of exploring on foot or by bike, here's what you need to know about navigating Yellowstone.

By Car

Driving is arguably the most popular and flexible way to explore Yellowstone. The park's roads are designed in a figure-eight loop, known as the Grand Loop Road, making it relatively easy to navigate between the major attractions. This iconic route connects you to the park's most famous landmarks, including Old Faithful, Yellowstone Lake, and the Grand Canyon of the Yellowstone. You can access the Grand Loop Road from any of the park's five entrances, allowing you to tailor your route based on where you're staying or which areas you want to prioritize. A seven-day pass to enter and drive in the park costs $35 per vehicle. Keep in mind that during peak season (June through August), traffic can be heavy, especially around popular attractions.

Shuttle Services

If you prefer to sit back and relax while someone else takes the wheel, Yellowstone offers various shuttle services. Guided tours are available, providing transportation while offering insights into the park's history, geology, and wildlife. These tours can be a great way to learn more about the park and enjoy the scenery without the stress of driving. Prices for these tours range from $40 to $100, depending on the route and duration.

By Bike

For those who want to experience Yellowstone at a slower pace and get some exercise while enjoying the scenery, biking is a fantastic option. The park has designated bike paths, and you can also cycle on the Grand Loop Road and other paved roads. Biking allows you to immerse yourself in the park's natural beauty and explore areas away from the main roads and crowds. If you need to rent a bike, rentals are available at various locations near the park's entrances, typically costing between $25 and $40 per day.

By Foot

Of course, no exploration of Yellowstone is complete without venturing out on foot. The park boasts over 1,000 miles of hiking trails, ranging from easy boardwalks to challenging backcountry treks. Hiking allows you to access areas that are inaccessible by car and experience the park's serenity and diverse ecosystems up close.

Whether you choose to explore Yellowstone by car, shuttle, bike, or on foot, remember to plan your routes, check for any road or trail closures, and be prepared for changing weather conditions. With a little planning, you'll be well-equipped to navigate this vast and awe-inspiring park.

CHAPTER 2: UNVEILING YELLOWSTONE'S SECRETS

A Brief History of Yellowstone

Yellowstone National Park isn't just a place you visit; it's a journey through time, a place where the Earth's ancient history is etched into the very landscape. As you stand amidst its geysers and canyons, you're walking in the footsteps of those who have marveled at its wonders for centuries. Millions of years ago, long before it became the world's first national park in 1872, Yellowstone was shaped by colossal volcanic eruptions. These eruptions left behind a massive caldera, a volcanic crater that remains active today, fueling the park's iconic geothermal features.

For centuries, Native American tribes, including the Shoshone, Crow, and Nez Perce, thrived in and around Yellowstone. They revered the land and its power, incorporating its geothermal features into their healing practices, spiritual rituals, and daily lives. In the early 19th century, European explorers began venturing into this uncharted territory. John Colter, a member of the Lewis and Clark Expedition, was among the first to witness Yellowstone's wonders, bringing back tales of hot springs, mud pots, and geysers that were initially met with disbelief.

It wasn't until the 1870s that the world truly recognized the significance of this unique landscape. The Hayden Expedition of 1871, led by artist and explorer Ferdinand V. Hayden, documented Yellowstone's geothermal features and wildlife, paving the way for its preservation.

In 1872, President Ulysses S. Grant signed the Yellowstone National Park Protection Act, establishing Yellowstone as the world's first national park. This landmark decision marked a turning point in conservation, setting a precedent for protecting natural wonders for generations to come.

Today, as you explore Yellowstone's vast wilderness, remember that you're not just visiting a national park; you're stepping into a living testament to the Earth's history. It's a place where the past and present intertwine, offering a glimpse into the powerful forces that have shaped this remarkable landscape

Lesser-Known Facts About Yellowstone

Yellowstone National Park is a land of iconic sights—the eruption of Old Faithful, the vibrant hues of the Grand Prismatic Spring, and the sweeping vistas of the Grand Canyon of the Yellowstone. But beyond these famous landmarks lie hidden gems and fascinating stories that often go unnoticed. As you explore this incredible park, keep an eye out for these lesser-known wonders that add another layer of intrigue to your Yellowstone adventure. Beneath the park's geysers and hot springs lies a slumbering giant—the Yellowstone Caldera, the largest super volcano on Earth. This ancient caldera, formed by massive eruptions thousands of years ago, is a constant reminder of the powerful forces shaping this dynamic landscape. While Old Faithful often steals the show, Yellowstone boasts over 500 geysers—more than any other place in the world combined! Some, like the Grand Prismatic Spring, are renowned for their vibrant colors, while others quietly bubble away, hidden among the park's vast forests and meadows.

Move over, Arizona! Yellowstone has its own spectacular Grand Canyon, a 20-mile stretch of dramatic cliffs and cascading waterfalls. The canyon's vibrant yellow and orange walls, sculpted by ancient volcanic activity, offer breathtaking views that rival its more famous counterpart. Yellowstone isn't just about geothermal wonders; it's also a haven for wildlife. The park boasts the largest concentration of mammals in the lower 48 states, with bison, elk, wolves, and grizzly bears roaming freely.

Believe it or not, the Yellowstone River once flowed in the opposite direction! Thousands of years ago, a massive geological shift caused by volcanic eruptions altered the river's course. While the river eventually returned to its current path, remnants of its ancient riverbed can still be found within the park. Yellowstone's history extends beyond its natural wonders. Archaeological evidence reveals that Native American tribes have inhabited the region for at least 11,000 years, leaving behind a rich cultural heritage. Venture into the park's Petrified Forest, and you'll encounter ancient trees that have turned to stone over millions of years. These petrified trees, some over 50 million years old, stand as silent witnesses to Yellowstone's prehistoric past.

As you explore Yellowstone, keep an eye out for these lesser-known wonders. They add depth and intrigue to your journey, revealing the park's hidden stories and showcasing the incredible diversity of this natural wonderland.

Why Visit Yellowstone in 2025?

Yellowstone National Park has always been a bucket-list destination, drawing millions of visitors from around the globe. But 2025 is shaping up to be an especially exciting year to experience this natural wonderland. Here's why:

Centennial Celebrations

In 2025, Yellowstone will commemorate the centennial anniversary of the 1929 General Plan, a pivotal moment in the park's history that shaped its development and preservation. The National Park Service (NPS) is likely to host special events, exhibits, and educational programs, offering a unique opportunity to delve deeper into Yellowstone's past and witness how careful planning continues to protect its natural beauty.

Enhanced Visitor Experiences

Yellowstone is committed to continually improving its visitor experience, and by 2025, you'll find some exciting updates. New visitor centers and improved accessibility features will make the park more welcoming and inclusive for everyone. The NPS is also implementing a Transportation Plan to modernize the park's transportation system, with more eco-friendly options like electric shuttle buses and better-developed bike paths.

New Wildlife Conservation Initiatives

Yellowstone's wildlife is a major draw for many visitors, and 2025 will see the launch of new initiatives under the Yellowstone Wildlife Conservation Program. These initiatives focus on protecting key species like wolves, bison, and grizzly bears through research, habitat restoration, and safe wildlife corridors.

Uncovering New Geological Insights

Beneath Yellowstone's iconic geothermal features lies a supervolcano, a source of ongoing geological research and discovery. In 2025, expect even more fascinating insights into the park's volcanic activity, geothermal pools, and seismic activity, thanks to ongoing studies and new technologies.

Special Events and Celebrations

Yellowstone's 2025 events calendar is brimming with opportunities to connect with the park in new ways. From guided ranger-led tours and wildlife-viewing excursions to educational events and celebrations tied to the National Park Service's Centennial, there will be no shortage of exciting activities. In 2025, Yellowstone will continue to be a place where history, conservation, and nature converge. Whether you're interested in the park's rich cultural heritage, its vibrant wildlife, or its geological marvels, this year promises to be an especially enriching time to visit. With new programs, ongoing conservation efforts, and a renewed focus on sustainability, 2025 is shaping up to be a banner year for Yellowstone.

CHAPTER 3: MUST-SEE ATTRACTIONS

Old Faithful Geyser and Other Hot Springs

Get ready to be amazed! Old Faithful, Yellowstone's most famous geyser, is a sight you won't soon forget. Imagine a towering column of water erupting from the earth, reaching heights of over 100 feet, with the roar of the eruption echoing through the surrounding landscape. It's a primal display of nature's power and beauty, and it's been captivating visitors for centuries. Old Faithful earned its name for its remarkable predictability. Eruptions occur roughly every 90 minutes, give or take, making it a reliable spectacle for eager onlookers. But don't just stand there waiting – the Upper Geyser Basin, where Old Faithful resides, is a geothermal wonderland with a plethora of other fascinating features to explore. Wander along the boardwalks that wind through the basin, and you'll encounter a mesmerizing array of geysers, hot springs, and fumaroles. Each one is unique, with its own personality and rhythm. Some erupt with a dramatic flourish, while others gently bubble and steam, creating a symphony of sights and sounds.

A Deeper Dive into Old Faithful

Old Faithful's history is intertwined with the very discovery of Yellowstone. Early explorers and Native American tribes were awestruck by this geyser, recognizing its power and mystique. Today, it remains a symbol of the park, drawing millions of visitors each year.

Location and Access

Old Faithful is located in the Upper Geyser Basin in the southwestern region of Yellowstone National Park, about 16 miles south of Madison Junction. It's easily accessible by car via the Grand Loop Road, with ample parking available nearby. You can also reach the area by taking the park's shuttle buses.

What to Do

- **Witness an Eruption:** Check the predicted eruption times posted at the Old Faithful Visitor Education Center and find a spot on the boardwalk to witness the spectacle. The anticipation builds as the geyser starts to rumble and steam, culminating in a magnificent display of water and power.
- **Explore the Boardwalks:** Take your time strolling along the boardwalks that meander through the Upper Geyser Basin. You'll encounter a variety of geysers, hot springs, and fumaroles, each with its own unique characteristics. Look for colorful pools like Morning Glory Pool and the vibrant hues of Chromatic Spring.
- **Observation Point Hike:** For a panoramic view, consider a hike up the Observation Point Trail. It's a moderate 1.6-mile (round-trip) hike that provides stunning views of Old Faithful and the surrounding geyser basin from an elevated perspective.

Where to Stay

- **Old Faithful Inn:** This historic inn, built in 1904, is an architectural marvel and offers a range of accommodations, from traditional rooms to suites with modern amenities. It's a great place to grab a bite to eat or simply soak in the atmosphere.
- **Old Faithful Snow Lodge & Cabins:** A more contemporary option with comfortable rooms and cabins, ideal for those seeking a modern lodging experience with easy access to Old Faithful.

What to Eat and Drink

- **Old Faithful Inn Dining Room:** This historic dining room offers a unique atmosphere with hearty meals and stunning views.
- **Bear Pit Lounge:** Located in the Old Faithful Snow Lodge, this lounge is a great spot for casual dining, snacks, and drinks.

- **Geyser Grill:** Enjoy classic American fare and grilled dishes at this casual restaurant near Old Faithful.

Essential Information

- **Best Time to Visit:** Old Faithful is a year-round attraction, but the summer months (June-September) offer the most predictable eruption patterns and the best weather for exploring the area.
- **Cost:** Included with your Yellowstone National Park entrance fee. The park entrance fee is $35 per vehicle for a 7-day pass.
- **Website:** Old Faithful and Yellowstone National Park Lodges
- **Time of Opening:** The Upper Geyser Basin is open 24 hours a day, but visitor centers and facilities have specific operating hours. The Old Faithful Visitor Center is typically open from 7:00 AM to 9:00 PM in peak season (June–September).
- **Additional Travel Information**: Be sure to wear comfortable shoes for walking on the boardwalks and bring layers of clothing as the weather can change quickly in Yellowstone. It's also a good idea to carry water and snacks, especially if you plan to spend several hours exploring the area.

Old Faithful and the Upper Geyser Basin offer a glimpse into the raw power and beauty of Yellowstone's geothermal wonders. It's an experience that will leave you in awe of nature's artistry and inspire a deeper connection to this remarkable park.

The Grand Prismatic Spring

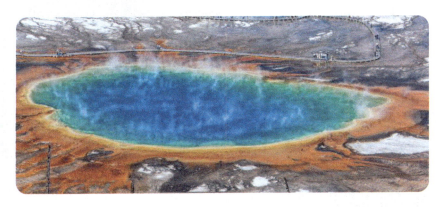

Prepare to have your breath taken away! The Grand Prismatic Spring is like stepping into a surreal, otherworldly landscape. Imagine a pool of water so vividly colored, it seems to defy the laws of nature. Deep blues, fiery oranges, radiant reds, and lush greens swirl together, creating a mesmerizing spectacle that will leave you speechless. This isn't just any hot spring; it's the largest in the United States and the third largest in the world. Its sheer size is impressive, but it's the kaleidoscope of colors that truly sets it apart. These vibrant hues are created by heat-loving microorganisms called thermophiles, which thrive in the spring's mineral-rich waters.

A Natural Masterpiece with a Colorful Past

The Grand Prismatic Spring has captivated visitors for centuries. Early explorers and Native American tribes were mesmerized by its beauty, weaving stories and legends around its vibrant colors. Today, it remains one of Yellowstone's most beloved and photographed attractions.

Location and Access

The Grand Prismatic Spring is located in the Midway Geyser Basin, a geothermal wonderland situated between the Upper and Lower Geyser Basins in the southwestern region of Yellowstone National Park.

You can easily reach it by car via the Grand Loop Road, with a designated parking area nearby. Alternatively, you can hop on one of the park's shuttle buses that service the Midway Geyser Basin.

What to Do

- **Marvel at the Colors:** Take a moment to simply soak in the beauty of the Grand Prismatic Spring. The vibrant hues are most intense on sunny days, so try to visit when the weather is clear.
- **Explore the Boardwalks:** Wander along the boardwalks that encircle the spring, offering different perspectives and vantage points. You'll also encounter other geothermal features in the Midway Geyser Basin, such as Excelsior Geyser and Turquoise Pool.
- **Hike to the Overlook:** For a truly breathtaking view, hike the short but steep trail to the Grand Prismatic Spring Overlook. From this elevated vantage point, you can appreciate the full scale of the spring and its mesmerizing colors.

Where to Stay

While there are no lodging options within the Midway Geyser Basin itself, you can find a variety of accommodations in nearby areas:

- **Old Faithful Inn and Cabins:** Located about a 15-minute drive from the Grand Prismatic Spring, this historic inn offers a range of lodging options with easy access to other geothermal features.
- **Old Faithful Snow Lodge & Cabins**: A more contemporary option with comfortable rooms and cabins, also situated near Old Faithful.
- **Grant Village:** This lodging area offers a variety of accommodations, including hotel rooms, cabins, and campgrounds, and is about a 20-minute drive from the Grand Prismatic Spring.

What to Eat and Drink

Since the Midway Geyser Basin is a day-use area, there are no restaurants or cafes on-site. However, you can find dining options at nearby lodging areas:

- **Old Faithful Inn Dining Room:** Enjoy a meal in this historic dining room with its grand atmosphere and views of Old Faithful.
- **Grant Village Dining Room:** This casual restaurant offers a variety of American and international cuisine.

- **Picnic Areas:** Pack a lunch and enjoy a picnic amidst the stunning scenery of the Midway Geyser Basin.

Essential Information

- **Best Time to Visit:** The Grand Prismatic Spring is a year-round attraction, but the summer months offer the most vibrant colors and the best weather for exploring the area.
- **Cost**: Included with your Yellowstone National Park entrance fee. The park entrance fee is $35 per vehicle for a 7-day pass.
- **Website**: Yellowstone National Park Lodges
- **Time of Opening:** The Midway Geyser Basin is open 24 hours a day, but visitor centers and facilities have specific operating hours.

Additional Travel Information: Be sure to wear comfortable shoes for walking on the boardwalks and bring layers of clothing as the weather can change quickly in Yellowstone. It's also a good idea to carry water and snacks, especially if you plan to spend several hours exploring the area.

The Grand Prismatic Spring is a true testament to the beauty and wonder of Yellowstone National Park. Its vibrant colors and otherworldly landscape will leave a lasting impression, inspiring awe and wonder in all who visit.

Yellowstone Lake

Imagine yourself standing on the shores of a crystal-clear lake, surrounded by towering mountains and the scent of fresh pine. The sun glistens on the water's surface, and a gentle breeze whispers through the trees. This is Yellowstone Lake, the largest high-elevation lake in North America, and a place where serenity meets the raw power of nature. Yellowstone Lake is not just a scenic wonder; it's a vital part of the park's ecosystem, teeming with life and geological wonders. Beneath its tranquil surface lie geothermal vents and hot springs, a reminder of the volcanic forces that shaped this landscape.

A Lake Born of Fire and Ice

Formed over 600,000 years ago by volcanic activity, Yellowstone Lake occupies a portion of the Yellowstone Caldera, a massive volcanic crater. Its history is intertwined with the park's geothermal wonders and the Native American tribes who have long relied on its abundance.

Location and Access

Yellowstone Lake is located in the heart of Yellowstone National Park, stretching across the southern and southeastern regions. It's easily accessible by car via the Grand Loop Road, with various pull-offs and viewpoints along its shores.

What to Do

- **Scenic Drives and Hikes:** Take a leisurely drive along the Grand Loop Road, stopping at scenic overlooks like Lake Butte Overlook and West Thumb Geyser Basin. For a more immersive experience, hike the Yellowstone Lake Overlook Trail or the Storm Point Trail, which offer stunning views and opportunities to spot wildlife.
- **Boating and Fishing:** Rent a boat or bring your own kayak or canoe to explore the lake's pristine waters. You can also cast a line and try your luck at fishing for cutthroat trout, lake trout, and other species. Remember to obtain a fishing permit before you go.
- **Wildlife Watching:** Keep your eyes peeled for wildlife along the lake's shores and surrounding forests. You might spot bison, elk, moose, or even grizzly bears. Bald eagles and ospreys often soar overhead, adding to the natural spectacle.
- **Relax and Unwind:** Find a peaceful spot along the shoreline and simply soak in the tranquility of Yellowstone Lake. The gentle lapping of waves, the fresh mountain air, and the stunning scenery create a sense of calm and wonder.

Where to Stay

- **Lake Yellowstone Hotel:** This historic hotel, built in 1891, offers elegant accommodations and stunning views of the lake. It's the perfect place to indulge in a bit of luxury amidst the wilderness.
- **Lake Lodge Cabins:** For a more rustic experience, consider staying in one of the charming cabins at Lake Lodge. These cabins offer a cozy retreat near the lake's shores.
- **Bridge Bay Campground:** If you prefer camping, Bridge Bay Campground offers a variety of campsites near the lake, allowing you to fall asleep to the sounds of nature.

What to Eat and Drink

- **Lake Yellowstone Hotel** Dining Room: Enjoy fine dining with panoramic lake views at this elegant restaurant.
- **Lake Lodge Cafeteria**: This casual cafeteria offers a variety of meals and snacks for those on the go.
- **Picnic Areas:** Pack a lunch and find a scenic spot along the lake to enjoy a picnic amidst the natural beauty.

Essential Information

- **Best Time to Visit:** Yellowstone Lake is accessible year-round, but the summer months offer the best weather for boating, fishing, and other activities.
- **Cost**: Included with your Yellowstone National Park entrance fee. The park entrance fee is $35 per vehicle for a 7-day pass.
- **Website:** Yellowstone National Park Lodges
- **Time of Opening:** The lake is open 24 hours a day, but visitor centers and facilities have specific operating hours.

Additional Travel Information: Be sure to bring layers of clothing, as the weather can change quickly near the lake. Sunscreen, sunglasses, and a hat are also recommended for sun protection.

Yellowstone Lake is a place of tranquility and natural wonder, offering a respite from the hustle and bustle of everyday life. Whether you're seeking adventure or relaxation, this iconic lake will leave you with a profound appreciation for the beauty and power of the natural world.

The Yellowstone River and Waterfalls

Imagine standing on the rim of a vibrant canyon, the ground trembling beneath your feet as the roar of a mighty waterfall fills the air. This is the Yellowstone River, the lifeblood of Yellowstone National Park, carving its way through the landscape and creating breathtaking waterfalls that have captivated visitors for centuries. The Yellowstone River is the longest undammed river in the contiguous United States, flowing for 692 miles from the Absaroka Mountains to the Missouri River. Its journey through Yellowstone is particularly dramatic, shaping the park's iconic Grand Canyon and giving rise to two magnificent waterfalls: the Upper Falls and the Lower Falls.

A River of Legends and History

The Yellowstone River has played a vital role in the history of the park, providing sustenance and transportation for Native American tribes and inspiring awe in early explorers. Today, it remains a symbol of the park's wild beauty and a testament to the power of nature.

Location and Access

The Yellowstone River flows through the heart of Yellowstone National Park, with its most dramatic features located in the Grand Canyon of the Yellowstone. You can access the canyon by car via the Grand Loop Road, with various viewpoints and trailheads along the South and North Rims.

What to Do

- **Witness the Majesty of the Falls:** Stand in awe of the Upper Falls, a 109-foot cascade of water, and the Lower Falls, a thundering 308-foot plunge that creates a misty spectacle.
- **Hike to Inspiration Point:** For a panoramic view of the canyon and the Lower Falls, hike the short but steep trail to Inspiration Point. The vista from here is simply breathtaking.
- **Explore the Brink of the Lower Falls:** If you're feeling adventurous, hike the Uncle Tom's Trail, which descends over 300 steps to the brink of the Lower Falls. You'll feel the mist on your face and witness the raw power of the waterfall up close.
- **Artist Point and Lookout Point**: These iconic viewpoints offer stunning perspectives of the Lower Falls and the canyon's colorful walls.
- **Red Rock Point:** For a different perspective, visit Red Rock Point, which provides views of the Upper Falls and the canyon from the North Rim.

Where to Stay

- **Canyon Lodge and Cabins:** Located near the Grand Canyon of the Yellowstone, Canyon Lodge offers a range of accommodations, from hotel rooms to cozy cabins.
- **Grant Village:** This lodging area offers a variety of accommodations, including hotel rooms, cabins, and a campground, and is about a 20-minute drive from the Grand Canyon of the Yellowstone.

What to Eat and Drink

- **Canyon Lodge Dining Room:** Enjoy casual dining with canyon views at this restaurant.
- **Grant Village Dining Room:** This restaurant offers a variety of American and international cuisine.
- **Picnic Areas:** Pack a lunch and find a scenic spot along the canyon rim to enjoy a picnic amidst the natural beauty.

Essential Information

- **Best Time to Visit:** The Yellowstone River and waterfalls are accessible year-round, but the summer months offer the best weather for hiking and exploring the canyon.

- **Cost:** Included with your Yellowstone National Park entrance fee. The park entrance fee is $35 per vehicle for a 7-day pass.
- **Website:** Yellowstone National Park Lodges
- **Time of Opening:** The Grand Canyon of the Yellowstone is open 24 hours a day, but visitor centers and facilities have specific operating hours.

Additional Travel Information: Be sure to wear comfortable shoes for hiking and bring layers of clothing as the weather can change quickly in the canyon. Sunscreen, sunglasses, and a hat are also recommended for sun protection.

The Yellowstone River and its magnificent waterfalls are a testament to the power and beauty of nature. As you stand on the canyon rim, feeling the mist on your face and hearing the roar of the falls, you'll be captivated by the raw energy and grandeur of this iconic landscape.

Lamar Valley

Imagine a place where bison graze in lush meadows, elk bugle their haunting calls, and wolves roam in packs. This is Lamar Valley, often called the "Serengeti of North America," a wildlife paradise nestled in the northeastern corner of Yellowstone National Park. Lamar Valley is a vast, open expanse, framed by towering mountains and carved by the winding Lamar River. Its diverse landscape provides a haven for a remarkable array of wildlife, making it a must-visit for any nature enthusiast.

A Haven for Wildlife Since Time Immemorial

For centuries, Lamar Valley has been a vital habitat for Yellowstone's iconic species. Native American tribes hunted here, and early explorers marveled at the abundance of wildlife. Today, it remains a critical ecosystem and a prime location for observing animals in their natural environment.

Location and Access

Lamar Valley is located in the northeastern region of Yellowstone National Park, accessible via the Grand Loop Road or the park's Northeast Entrance. The drive to the valley is scenic, with opportunities to spot wildlife along the way.

What to Do

- **Wildlife Watching:** Lamar Valley is renowned for its exceptional wildlife viewing opportunities. Bring your binoculars and spotting scope to observe bison herds grazing in the meadows, elk bugling during the fall rut, and wolves hunting in packs. Early mornings and evenings are the best times to spot wildlife.
- **Scenic Drives and Hikes**: Take a leisurely drive through the valley, stopping at pullouts and overlooks to soak in the scenery. For a more immersive experience, hike the Lamar Valley Trail or the Specimen Ridge Trail, which offer stunning views and opportunities for solitude.
- **Photography:** Lamar Valley is a photographer's dream, with its wide-open landscapes, dramatic lighting, and abundant wildlife. Capture the essence of Yellowstone's wild beauty with your camera.
- **Picnicking:** Pack a lunch and find a scenic spot along the Lamar River to enjoy a picnic amidst the natural beauty.

Where to Stay

- **Mammoth Hot Springs Hotel and Cabins:** Located about a 45-minute drive from Lamar Valley, Mammoth Hot Springs Hotel offers a range of accommodations, from historic rooms to modern cabins.
- **Roosevelt Lodge & Cabins:** This rustic lodge offers a unique Western experience, with horseback riding and stagecoach rides available.
- **Cooke City and Silver Gate:** These nearby towns offer a variety of lodging options, from cozy cabins to motels, just outside the park's Northeast Entrance.

What to Eat and Drink

- **Mammoth Hot Springs Dining Room:** Enjoy casual dining with a variety of American cuisine at this restaurant.
- **Roosevelt Lodge Dining Room:** This rustic dining room offers hearty meals and a Western atmosphere.
- **Cooke City and Silver Gate Restaurants:** Explore the local dining scene in these nearby towns, with options ranging from cafes to steakhouses.

Essential Information

- **Best Time to Visit:** Lamar Valley is accessible year-round, but the summer months offer the best weather for wildlife viewing and hiking. Fall is also a great time to visit, as the elk rut creates a dramatic spectacle.
- **Cost:** Included with your Yellowstone National Park entrance fee. The park entrance fee is $35 per vehicle for a 7-day pass.
- **Website:** Yellowstone National Park
- **Time of Opening:** Lamar Valley is open 24 hours a day, but visitor centers and facilities have specific operating hours.

Additional Travel Information: Be sure to bring binoculars or a spotting scope for wildlife viewing, and dress in layers as the weather can change quickly in the valley. Sunscreen, sunglasses, and a hat are also recommended for sun protection.

Lamar Valley is a true testament to the wild beauty and abundant wildlife of Yellowstone National Park. As you immerse yourself in its vast landscapes and observe the animals that call it home, you'll experience a profound connection to the natural world.

CHAPTER 4: DINING AND SHOPPING

Best Restaurants and Cafes in Yellowstone

After a day of exploring Yellowstone's breathtaking scenery and wildlife encounters, you'll undoubtedly work up an appetite. Luckily, the park offers a delightful array of dining options to satisfy every craving, from hearty meals with a view to casual grab-and-go snacks. Here are some of the best restaurants and cafes to check out during your Yellowstone adventure:

Old Faithful Inn Dining Room

- Location: Old Faithful Area
- Type: Upscale American Cuisine
- Phone: +1 307-545-3310
- Website: Old Faithful Inn Dining Room

Step into the grandeur of the Old Faithful Inn Dining Room, where towering log walls and massive stone fireplaces create a rustic yet elegant ambiance. Savor regional dishes like bison and trout while enjoying views of the iconic Old Faithful geyser. Reservations are highly recommended, especially during peak season.

Lake Yellowstone Hotel Dining Room

- Location: Lake Yellowstone Area
- Type: Fine Dining, Contemporary American
- Phone: +1 307-344-7311
- Website: Lake Yellowstone Hotel Dining Room

Indulge in a refined dining experience at the Lake Yellowstone Hotel Dining Room, where panoramic views of the serene lake accompany a menu of locally sourced ingredients and contemporary American cuisine. Be sure to make reservations in advance, as this popular dining spot fills up quickly.

Canyon Lodge Dining Room

- Location: Canyon Village Area
- Type: Family-Friendly Dining, American Cuisine
- Phone: +1 307-344-7311
- Website: Canyon Lodge Dining Room

After a day of exploring the Grand Canyon of the Yellowstone, unwind at the Canyon Lodge Dining Room. This family-friendly restaurant offers a relaxed atmosphere with classic American comfort food like fried chicken and hearty salads.

Mammoth Hot Springs Dining Room

- Location: Mammoth Hot Springs Area
- Type: Buffet, Classic American
- Phone: +1 307-344-7311

Conveniently located near the park's North Entrance, the Mammoth Hot Springs Dining Room is a great option for a quick and satisfying meal. Enjoy a buffet-style selection of classic American dishes, perfect for fueling up after a day of sightseeing.

The Bear Pit Lounge

- Location: Old Faithful Area
- Type: Casual Dining, Pub Fare
- Phone: +1 307-545-3030

For a more laid-back dining experience, head to The Bear Pit Lounge at the Old Faithful Snow Lodge. This casual lounge offers a variety of pub fare, from bison burgers to fish tacos, along with local beers and cocktails.

Additional Dining Tips

- **Make Reservations:** For popular restaurants, especially during peak season, it's highly recommended to make reservations in advance.
- **Pack Snacks:** If you're planning on spending the day hiking or exploring remote areas, be sure to pack snacks and water, as dining options may be limited.
- **Check for Seasonal Hours:** Some restaurants and cafes may have limited hours or be closed during the off-season.
- **Explore Local Options:** If you're venturing outside the park, explore the dining scene in nearby towns like West Yellowstone and Gardiner, where you'll find a variety of local restaurants and cafes.

With its diverse range of dining options, Yellowstone ensures that you'll find the perfect place to refuel and savor delicious meals amidst the park's stunning scenery.

Grocery Stores and Local Markets

Whether you're planning a picnic lunch, stocking up on snacks for your hikes, or simply craving a taste of local flavor, Yellowstone National Park and its surrounding communities offer a variety of grocery stores and markets to meet your needs. Here's a guide to help you find the essentials and discover some unique treats along the way:

Inside Yellowstone

Each of Yellowstone's main developed areas has a general store where you can find basic groceries, camping supplies, and souvenirs. These stores are perfect for grabbing those last-minute items or replenishing your supplies during your trip. Expect to find essentials like bread, milk, eggs, snacks, and some pre-packaged meals. You'll also find camping gear, sunscreen, insect repellent, and those all-important Yellowstone souvenirs.

Beyond the Park

The towns bordering Yellowstone offer a wider selection of grocery stores and markets, often with a focus on local and regional products. West Yellowstone, Montana, just outside the West Entrance, boasts several markets with fresh produce, locally sourced meats and cheeses, and delicious baked goods. Be sure to try the huckleberry jam, a regional favorite!

Gardiner and Livingston, Montana, near the North Entrance, offer small-town grocery stores with a charming atmosphere. You'll find unique regional products, like handmade goods and local honey, alongside your everyday essentials.

On-the-Go Snacks

If you find yourself needing a quick bite or a drink while exploring the park, stop by the Fishing Bridge General Store. This convenient location offers pre-packaged snacks, drinks, and simple meals like sandwiches and hot dogs.

Eco-Friendly Options

Yellowstone is committed to sustainability, and many local markets in and around the park reflect this ethos. Look for stores offering eco-friendly products, such as reusable bags, biodegradable soaps, and local, organic produce. You can enjoy your visit while minimizing your environmental impact.

Tips for Grocery Shopping in Yellowstone

- **Plan Ahead:** If you're staying in a cabin or planning on cooking your own meals, make a list of essentials before you arrive.
- **Check Store Hours:** Some stores may have limited hours, especially during the off-season.
- **Bring Reusable Bags:** Help reduce waste by bringing your own reusable bags for your groceries.
- **Support Local Businesses:** When possible, choose local markets and stores to support the communities surrounding Yellowstone.

With a little planning, you'll find everything you need to enjoy delicious meals and snacks during your Yellowstone adventure. Whether you're picnicking by a scenic lake or stocking up for a backcountry hike, these grocery stores and local markets have you covered.

Souvenirs and Gifts to Bring Home

As your Yellowstone adventure draws to a close, you'll want to take home a piece of the magic to cherish the memories. Luckily, the park offers a delightful array of souvenirs and gifts, from classic apparel and local handicrafts to unique treasures that capture the essence of this natural wonderland. Here's a guide to help you find the perfect mementos to commemorate your Yellowstone experience:

Yellowstone National Park Apparel

What better way to show your love for Yellowstone than with a stylish and practical piece of clothing? Whether it's a cozy hoodie for those chilly evenings or a classic t-shirt featuring the iconic park logo, Yellowstone apparel is a popular choice for visitors of all ages.

Locally Made Handicrafts and Artwork

Yellowstone is home to many talented artisans who create unique, handcrafted goods that reflect the park's beauty and spirit. Browse for intricately beaded jewelry, pottery with nature-inspired designs, or stunning prints and paintings capturing Yellowstone's iconic landscapes. These one-of-a-kind souvenirs are a great way to support local artists and bring home a piece of Yellowstone's creative spirit.

Yellowstone-Themed Books and Educational Materials

For those who love to learn and delve deeper into the park's history and natural wonders, consider picking up a book about Yellowstone. From field guides that help you identify local flora and fauna to captivating stories and historical accounts, these books offer a way to continue your Yellowstone journey long after you've returned home.

Yellowstone-Scented Candles and Soaps

Bring the essence of Yellowstone into your home with beautifully crafted scented candles and soaps. These delightful souvenirs capture the park's natural aromas, from the fresh scent of pine forests to the soothing fragrance of wildflowers. Each time you light a candle or use a bar of soap, you'll be transported back to the serenity of Yellowstone's landscapes.

Eco-Friendly Souvenirs

Show your support for Yellowstone's commitment to sustainability by choosing eco-friendly souvenirs. Look for reusable water bottles adorned with the park's logo, or durable tote bags made from recycled materials. These practical and environmentally conscious souvenirs are a great way to reduce waste and contribute to the park's conservation efforts.

Yellowstone-Themed Food and Snacks

Don't forget to savor the flavors of Yellowstone with some delicious treats to take home. Local shops offer a variety of Yellowstone-themed snacks, such as bison jerky and huckleberry jam. These tasty souvenirs are perfect for sharing with friends and family or enjoying as a reminder of your Yellowstone adventure.

Tips for Souvenir Shopping

- **Shop Local:** Support local artisans and businesses by purchasing handcrafted items and unique souvenirs from shops in and around the park.
- **Choose Quality:** Look for souvenirs that are well-made and will last, ensuring that your memories of Yellowstone endure.
- **Consider Practicality:** Select souvenirs that you'll actually use or display, so they can serve as a constant reminder of your trip.
- **Set a Budget:** It's easy to get carried away with souvenir shopping, so set a budget beforehand to avoid overspending.

CHAPTER 5: OUTDOOR ACTIVITIES AND ADVENTURES

Hiking Trails for All Skill Levels

Yellowstone National Park is a hiker's paradise, with over 1,000 miles of trails winding through its diverse landscapes. Whether you're a seasoned hiker or just starting out, there's a trail for you in Yellowstone.

Easy Trails

- **Upper Geyser Basin Loop**: This 1.5-mile loop takes you past some of Yellowstone's most famous geothermal features, including Old Faithful and Castle Geyser. The boardwalks make it easy to explore the area, and the trail is mostly flat and accessible.
- **West Thumb Geyser Basin**: Located along the southern shore of Yellowstone Lake, this 0.7-mile boardwalk trail offers stunning views of both the geothermal pools and the lake. It's an easy walk with minimal elevation gain, making it a great option for families with young children.
- **Lamar River Trail:** This 2-mile trail follows the Lamar River, known for its wildlife sightings. It's a relatively flat and easy trail, perfect for those who want to enjoy a leisurely stroll while keeping an eye out for bison, elk, and other wildlife.

Moderate Trails

- **Mystic Falls Trail:** This 2.4-mile round-trip trail takes you to the beautiful Mystic Falls, a hidden gem in the Upper Geyser Basin. The trail is moderately steep in some sections, but the views of the falls and the surrounding landscape are worth the effort.
- **Mount Washburn Trail:** For panoramic views of Yellowstone, the Mount Washburn Trail is a must-do. This 6.2-mile round-trip hike takes you to the summit of Mount Washburn, where you'll be rewarded with sweeping vistas of the park's valleys, geothermal features, and even the Grand Teton Range in the distance.

Difficult Trails

- **The Yellowstone River Trail:** This 6.5-mile (one-way) trail follows the Yellowstone River, offering stunning views of the canyon and the surrounding wilderness. It's a strenuous hike with significant elevation changes, so be prepared for a challenge.
- **Crested Pool to Pelican Valley:** This 10-mile hike takes you through Yellowstone's backcountry to one of its most remote valleys. You'll pass through meadows, forests, and geothermal areas, with the chance to see a variety of wildlife. This trail is best for experienced hikers who are comfortable with backcountry navigation.

Tips for Hiking in Yellowstone

- **Plan Your Hike**: Choose a trail that matches your fitness level and experience. Check the park's website or visitor centers for trail conditions and any closures.
- **Be Prepared:** Wear sturdy hiking boots, dress in layers, and bring plenty of water and snacks.
- **Carry Bear Spray:** Yellowstone is bear country, so it's essential to carry bear spray and know how to use it.
- **Stay on Marked Trails:** Avoid wandering off the trails to protect yourself and the fragile ecosystem.
- **Respect Wildlife:** Observe wildlife from a safe distance and never approach or feed animals.

With its diverse range of trails, Yellowstone offers hiking experiences for everyone. Whether you're seeking a leisurely stroll or a challenging adventure, you'll find the perfect path to explore the park's natural wonders.

Wildlife Watching

Yellowstone National Park is a wildlife enthusiast's dream, a place where you can witness animals roaming freely in their natural habitat. From the majestic bison to the elusive wolf, the park offers a chance to connect with the wild side of the American West.

What to Expect
Yellowstone is home to an incredible diversity of wildlife, including:

- **Bison:** These massive creatures are a symbol of the park, often seen grazing in meadows or crossing roads.
- **Elk**: Keep an eye out for elk, especially during the fall rutting season when the males' bugling calls echo through the valleys.
- **Grizzly Bears:** Yellowstone is one of the few places in the U.S. where you can see grizzly bears in the wild. Remember to always maintain a safe distance.
- **Wolves:** The reintroduction of wolves in the 1990s has been a conservation success story. Lamar Valley is a prime spot for wolf watching.
- **Other Wildlife:** You might also spot moose, bighorn sheep, pronghorn antelope, and a variety of birds.

Where to Go for the Best Wildlife Viewing

- **Lamar Valley:** Often called the "Serengeti of North America," Lamar Valley is a must-visit for wildlife enthusiasts.
- **Hayden Valley:** Another prime spot for wildlife, Hayden Valley is located between Canyon Village and Fishing Bridge.
- **Mammoth Hot Springs:** This area is known for its elk population, especially during the fall rut.
- **Yellowstone Lake:** Look for moose and bald eagles near the lake's shores.

Tips for Wildlife Watching

- **Timing is Key:** Early mornings and late evenings are generally the best times to see wildlife.
- **Bring Binoculars:** A good pair of binoculars or a spotting scope will enhance your viewing experience.
- **Respect the Animals:** Always maintain a safe distance from wildlife and never approach or feed them.
- **Be Patient:** Wildlife sightings are not guaranteed, so be patient and enjoy the beauty of your surroundings.
- **Attend Ranger Programs:** Park rangers often lead wildlife watching tours and offer valuable insights.

With its diverse habitats and abundant wildlife, Yellowstone offers a unique opportunity to connect with nature and witness animals in their natural splendor. Remember to be respectful, patient, and prepared, and you'll be rewarded with unforgettable wildlife encounters.

Scenic Drives

Yellowstone National Park is a land of dramatic landscapes, where towering mountains meet sprawling valleys, pristine lakes reflect the sky, and geothermal wonders dot the terrain. One of the best ways to experience this diverse beauty is by embarking on a scenic drive. Here are some of the most unforgettable routes to explore:

The Grand Loop Road

This 142-mile loop is the main artery of Yellowstone, connecting many of the park's most iconic attractions. As you traverse this route, you'll witness the eruption of Old Faithful, marvel at the colorful Grand Prismatic Spring, and gaze upon the grandeur of the Grand Canyon of the Yellowstone. Allow ample time for this drive, as you'll want to stop frequently to soak in the views and explore the many wonders along the way.

Beartooth Highway

For a truly breathtaking experience, venture onto the Beartooth Highway, a 68-mile stretch of road that climbs to over 10,000 feet, offering panoramic vistas of snow-capped peaks, alpine meadows, and crystal-clear lakes. This All-American Road is a must-do for those seeking adventure and unparalleled scenery.

Yellowstone Lake Loop

Embrace the tranquility of Yellowstone Lake with a scenic drive along its 30-mile shoreline. You'll encounter geothermal features at West Thumb Geyser Basin, charming lakeside villages, and the historic Fishing Bridge, a prime spot for birdwatching.

Grand Teton Scenic Byway

If you're entering Yellowstone from the south, don't miss the opportunity to drive the Grand Teton Scenic Byway. This 43-mile route winds through Grand Teton National Park, offering majestic views of the Teton Range, with its jagged peaks rising dramatically above the valley floor.

Winter Scenic Drives

Even in winter, Yellowstone's scenic drives offer a unique perspective of the park's snow-covered landscapes. Join a guided snowmobile or snow coach tour to access areas that are closed to regular vehicles and witness the park's geothermal features and wildlife amidst a winter wonderland.

Tips for Scenic Drives in Yellowstone

- Plan Your Route: Yellowstone is vast, so plan your drives in advance, considering your interests and time constraints.
- Check Road Conditions: Be aware of road closures and construction, especially during the shoulder seasons.
- Fill Up Your Gas Tank: Gas stations are limited within the park, so ensure you have enough fuel for your journeys.
- Pack for All Weather: Yellowstone's weather can be unpredictable, so be prepared for sudden changes with layers of clothing and rain gear.
- Take Your Time: Don't rush your scenic drives. Stop frequently to admire the views, take photos, and explore the many wonders along the way.

With its diverse landscapes and breathtaking scenery, Yellowstone offers a scenic driving experience unlike any other. So, buckle up, roll down the windows, and prepare to be amazed by the beauty that unfolds before you.

Boating, Fishing, and Water Sports

Yellowstone National Park isn't just about geysers and wildlife; it's also a haven for water enthusiasts. With pristine lakes, rivers, and streams, the park offers a refreshing escape and a chance to connect with nature in a whole new way. Whether you dream of casting a line in a crystal-clear lake or paddling through serene waters surrounded by breathtaking scenery, Yellowstone has something for everyone.

Boating on Yellowstone Lake

Yellowstone Lake is the crown jewel of the park's waterways, and boating is one of the best ways to experience its vastness and beauty. Rent a motorboat for an exhilarating ride or opt for a kayak or canoe for a more peaceful exploration. You can even embark on a scenic boat tour with a knowledgeable guide who will share fascinating insights about the lake's history, geology, and wildlife.

Fishing in Yellowstone's Waters

For anglers, Yellowstone is a paradise. The park's rivers and lakes teem with a variety of fish, including the native cutthroat trout. Whether you prefer fly fishing in a rushing river or casting a line from the shore of a peaceful lake, you're sure to find the perfect spot to test your skills and connect with nature.

Remember to obtain a fishing permit before you cast your line, and familiarize yourself with the park's fishing regulations to ensure a responsible and sustainable experience.

Kayaking, Canoeing, and Paddleboarding

For a more intimate experience on the water, consider kayaking, canoeing, or paddleboarding. These activities allow you to explore Yellowstone's waterways at your own pace, getting up close to the shoreline and soaking in the tranquility of the surroundings. Paddle through secluded coves, admire the reflections of the mountains on the water's surface, and keep an eye out for wildlife along the banks.

Winter Water Activities

Even in winter, Yellowstone's waterways offer unique opportunities for adventure. While boating and fishing are limited during the colder months, you can try ice fishing in designated areas or embark on a snowshoeing or cross-country skiing excursion along the frozen shores of Yellowstone Lake.

Tips for Water Activities in Yellowstone

- Safety First: Always wear a life jacket when boating, and be aware of changing weather conditions. Water temperatures can be cold, even in summer.
- Respect Wildlife: Maintain a safe distance from wildlife you encounter near the water, and avoid disturbing their natural habitat.
- Permits and Regulations: Obtain the necessary permits for fishing and boating, and familiarize yourself with the park's regulations to ensure a responsible visit.
- Plan Ahead: If you plan to rent equipment, make reservations in advance, especially during peak season.
- Pack Accordingly: Bring sunscreen, sunglasses, a hat, and layers of clothing to protect yourself from the elements.

With its pristine waterways and diverse range of activities, Yellowstone offers a refreshing escape for water enthusiasts. Whether you're seeking adventure or relaxation, the park's lakes and rivers provide a unique opportunity to connect with nature and create lasting memories.

Winter Activities in Yellowstone

When the snow blankets Yellowstone National Park, it transforms into a magical winter wonderland, offering a unique and serene experience unlike any other season. While the crowds diminish and some roads close, the park opens up a whole new realm of adventures for those who embrace the cold.

Snowshoeing and Cross-Country Skiing

Imagine gliding through silent forests, the only sound the soft crunch of snow beneath your feet. Yellowstone's winter trails beckon, offering miles of pristine landscapes to explore. Whether you prefer the leisurely pace of snowshoeing or the invigorating glide of cross-country skiing, you'll find trails for all skill levels. Some popular options include the Upper Geyser Basin Loop, where you can witness Old Faithful erupting amidst a snowy backdrop, or the Lamar Valley, where you might spot wolves and bison against the white expanse.

Snowmobiling

For a thrilling adventure, hop on a snowmobile and explore Yellowstone's winter wonderland with a guided tour. These tours offer access to areas that are inaccessible by car during the winter months, allowing you to venture deep into the park's backcountry and witness its hidden gems.

Wildlife Watching in Winter

Winter offers a unique opportunity for wildlife viewing. Animals like bison, elk, and wolves are often easier to spot against the snow, and their behaviors change as they adapt to the colder conditions. Join a ranger-led wildlife watching tour or venture out on your own to observe these magnificent creatures in their winter habitat.

Winter Photography

The combination of snow, steam, and dramatic lighting creates a photographer's paradise in Yellowstone's winter. Capture the ethereal beauty of geysers erupting against a frosty backdrop, or the stark contrast of wildlife against the white expanse.

Additional Winter Activities

- Ice Fishing: Try your hand at ice fishing in designated areas of Yellowstone Lake.
- Ranger Programs: Participate in ranger-led programs to learn about winter ecology, wildlife tracking, and the park's history.
- Soaking in Hot Springs: After a day of winter adventures, relax and rejuvenate in one of the park's natural hot springs.

Tips for Winter Activities

- Dress Warmly: Layers are essential for staying comfortable in Yellowstone's winter weather.
- Check Conditions: Be aware of road closures and trail conditions before heading out.
- Safety First: Let someone know your plans, carry bear spray, and be prepared for changing weather conditions.
- Embrace the Serenity: Winter in Yellowstone offers a unique sense of peace and tranquility. Take time to appreciate the quiet beauty of the park's frozen landscapes.

With its pristine scenery and unique winter adventures, Yellowstone National Park offers an unforgettable experience for those who embrace the cold. So, bundle up, explore the trails, and witness the magic of this winter wonderland.

CHAPTER 6: CRAFTING YOUR YELLOWSTONE ITINERARY

1-Day Itinerary

If you only have one day to spend in Yellowstone National Park, you'll want to make the most of it! This itinerary focuses on some of the park's most iconic sights and offers a taste of the diverse experiences Yellowstone has to offer.

Morning:

- Enter the park through the South Entrance and head towards West Thumb Geyser Basin.
- Take a stroll along the boardwalks of West Thumb Geyser Basin, marveling at the colorful hot springs and geysers nestled along the shores of Yellowstone Lake.
- Soak in the views of Yellowstone Lake, the largest high-elevation lake in North America.

Midday:

- Continue north to the Midway Geyser Basin and witness the awe-inspiring Grand Prismatic Spring, a massive hot spring with vibrant rainbow-like colors.
- Enjoy lunch at the Lake Yellowstone Hotel Dining Room, savoring delicious food with panoramic lake views.

Afternoon:

- Head to the Upper Geyser Basin and witness the legendary Old Faithful erupt. Check the predicted eruption times for the most accurate schedule.
- Take a short hike on the boardwalk trails around Old Faithful to see other geysers and hot springs in the area.
- Drive to the Grand Canyon of the Yellowstone and be awestruck by the Lower Falls, a 308-foot waterfall that plunges into the canyon.

Evening:

- As the day winds down, head towards Mammoth Hot Springs.
- Take a walk on the boardwalks around Mammoth Hot Springs, admiring the unique travertine terraces formed by the hot springs.
- Enjoy dinner at the Mammoth Hot Springs Dining Room, savoring a delicious meal in a historic setting.
- If you're staying overnight, consider lodging options in the Mammoth Hot Springs area or nearby Gardiner, Montana.

3-Day Itinerary

With three days in Yellowstone National Park, you can embark on a more immersive journey, exploring its diverse landscapes, witnessing iconic geothermal features, and encountering the park's abundant wildlife. This itinerary offers a balanced approach to experiencing Yellowstone's highlights while leaving room for spontaneous discoveries.

Day 1: Geothermal Wonders and Scenic Beauty

- Begin your day at the West Entrance, passing through the historic Roosevelt Arch, a symbol of Yellowstone's legacy. Make your way to the Upper Geyser Basin, a geothermal wonderland teeming with activity.
- Witness the eruption of Old Faithful, Yellowstone's most famous geyser, and stroll along the boardwalks to admire the colorful hot springs and geysers. Be sure to check the predicted eruption times posted near the visitor center.
- Embark on a moderate hike on the Fairy Falls Trail, which leads to a stunning overlook of the Grand Prismatic Spring, a massive hot spring with vibrant rainbow hues. This 5.2-mile (round-trip) hike takes you through lodgepole pine forests and past other geothermal features.

- In the afternoon, head south to the Midway Geyser Basin and marvel at the Excelsior Geyser, a powerful hot spring that roars and steams. Take in the sights and sounds of this dynamic geothermal area.
- As the day ends, find a peaceful spot along the Firehole River to watch the sunset over the meadows and reflect on the day's geothermal wonders.

Day 2: Waterfalls, Wildlife, and the Grand Canyon

- Start your day at the Grand Canyon of the Yellowstone, a breathtaking natural wonder with towering cliffs and cascading waterfalls. Take in the panoramic views from Artist Point and Lookout Point, marveling at the Lower Falls, a 308-foot waterfall that plunges into the canyon.
- Hike a portion of the South Rim Trail, a moderate 3-mile (round-trip) trail that offers stunning views of the canyon and the Yellowstone River. Consider hiking to Point Sublime for a different perspective.
- In the afternoon, venture to Lamar Valley, known for its abundant wildlife. Keep your binoculars handy for spotting bison, elk, and possibly even wolves or grizzly bears. Look for herds grazing in the meadows or near the Lamar River.
- As dusk settles, find a quiet spot in Lamar Valley and listen to the haunting bugle calls of elk during their mating season. The valley's open landscape provides excellent opportunities for wildlife photography.

Day 3: Exploring the Northern Reaches and Saying Farewell

- Begin your day with a scenic drive along the Grand Loop Road, heading north towards Mammoth Hot Springs. Stop at the Roaring Mountain, a geothermal area with steaming fumaroles, and take in the views of the surrounding mountains.
- Explore the Mammoth Hot Springs Terraces, a unique landscape of travertine formations created by the flow of hot springs. Walk the boardwalks and admire the colorful terraces and steaming pools.
- Visit the Albright Visitor Center and Museum to learn about the park's history, geology, and wildlife. Discover the stories of early explorers, Native American tribes, and the park's conservation efforts.
- In the afternoon, consider a moderate 6.4-mile (round-trip) hike to the summit of Mount Washburn for panoramic views of the park. From the summit, you can see the Grand Canyon of the Yellowstone, Yellowstone Lake, and the surrounding mountain ranges.

As your three-day adventure comes to a close, reflect on the diverse landscapes, geothermal wonders, and wildlife encounters that have made your Yellowstone experience unforgettable. Take a final scenic drive through a different section of the park, savoring the memories you've created.

This 3-day itinerary offers a more in-depth exploration of Yellowstone National Park, allowing you to experience its iconic sights, diverse landscapes, and abundant wildlife. With careful planning and a spirit of adventure, you're sure to create memories that will last a lifetime.

7-Day Itinerary

With a full week to explore Yellowstone National Park, you can embark on an unforgettable journey, immersing yourself in its diverse landscapes, witnessing its geothermal wonders, and encountering its abundant wildlife. This 7-day itinerary offers a comprehensive exploration of the park's highlights, with opportunities for both iconic sights and off-the-beaten-path discoveries.

Day 1: Arrival and Southern Delights

- Arrive at the South Entrance and begin your Yellowstone adventure.
- Head to West Thumb Geyser Basin, where you'll find colorful hot springs and geysers nestled along the shores of Yellowstone Lake.
- Take a scenic drive around Yellowstone Lake, stopping at overlooks to admire the views and soak in the tranquility.
- In the afternoon, visit the Grand Prismatic Spring, a massive hot spring with vibrant rainbow hues. Consider hiking the Fairy Falls Trail for a panoramic view.
- As evening approaches, make your way to Old Faithful and witness its iconic eruption. Explore the surrounding Upper Geyser Basin and its many geothermal features.
- Stay overnight at the Old Faithful Inn or Snow Lodge, immersing yourself in the park's historic atmosphere.

Day 2: Geysers, Basins, and Mammoth Hot Springs

- Start your day with a visit to the Black Sand Basin and Biscuit Basin, where you'll find more unique geothermal features.
- Head north to Norris Geyser Basin, one of the hottest and most active geothermal areas in the park. Witness the unpredictable Steamboat Geyser and explore the colorful Porcelain Basin.
- In the afternoon, hike to the Artist Paint Pots, a colorful collection of mud pots and hot springs.
- Continue to Mammoth Hot Springs and marvel at the travertine terraces, a stunning display of nature's artistry.
- Stay overnight at the Mammoth Hot Springs Hotel, enjoying the historic charm and convenient location.

Day 3: The Grand Canyon of the Yellowstone

- Spend the day exploring the Grand Canyon of the Yellowstone, a breathtaking natural wonder with towering cliffs and cascading waterfalls.
- Hike to the Lower Falls or take the South Rim Trail for magnificent views of the canyon and the Yellowstone River.
- Visit the Upper Falls and enjoy the panoramic vista from Artist Point.
- In the afternoon, relax and enjoy the scenery at Canyon Village, or consider a scenic boat ride on Yellowstone Lake.
- Stay overnight at Canyon Lodge or Canyon Campground, immersing yourself in the beauty of the canyon.

Day 4: Wildlife Watching in Lamar Valley

- Embark on a wildlife-watching adventure in Lamar Valley, known as the "Serengeti of North America."
- Rise early for the best chance to spot bison, wolves, elk, and grizzly bears in their natural habitat.
- Explore the valley's diverse landscapes, from open meadows to forested hillsides, and keep your eyes peeled for wildlife.
- Visit Slough Creek, another prime spot for wildlife sightings, and enjoy a picnic lunch amidst the scenery.
- In the afternoon, drive to the Northeast Entrance area and hike to Tower Fall, a picturesque waterfall cascading into the Yellowstone River.
- Stay overnight in Mammoth Hot Springs or the nearby town of Gardiner, enjoying the local charm and hospitality.

Day 5: Yellowstone Lake and West Thumb

- Spend the day exploring the wonders of Yellowstone Lake, the largest high-elevation lake in North America.
- Take a scenic boat tour on the lake, or hike the Yellowstone Lake Overlook Trail for panoramic views.
- Visit the Lake Yellowstone Hotel, a historic landmark with elegant architecture and stunning lakefront views.
- In the afternoon, explore the West Thumb Geyser Basin, a unique geothermal area located on the shores of the lake.
- Enjoy a relaxing evening at the Lake Yellowstone Hotel or Lake Lodge, savoring the tranquility of the lakeside setting.

Day 6: Northern Adventures and Hidden Gems

- Venture to the northern reaches of Yellowstone and discover some of the park's lesser-known treasures.
- Visit Bison Flats and Tower-Roosevelt for more opportunities to spot wildlife, including bison and wolves.
- Explore the Norris Geyser Basin, a dynamic geothermal area with a variety of geysers, hot springs, and fumaroles. Don't miss the Porcelain Basin and the Norris Museum.
- In the afternoon, consider a hike to the summit of Electric Peak, the highest point in the Gallatin Range, for breathtaking views.
- Enjoy a farewell dinner at the Mammoth Hot Springs Dining Room, reflecting on your week of Yellowstone adventures.

Day 7: Departure and Lasting Memories

- As your Yellowstone journey comes to an end, take a final scenic drive through the park, savoring the memories you've created.
- Visit Artist Point for a last glimpse of the Grand Canyon of the Yellowstone, and enjoy a leisurely breakfast at the Mammoth Hot Springs Hotel.
- If time allows, stop at Mud Volcano, a fascinating geothermal area with bubbling mud pots and steaming fumaroles.
- Depart from the park, carrying with you the awe-inspiring sights, sounds, and experiences of Yellowstone National Park.

This 7-day itinerary offers a comprehensive exploration of Yellowstone's wonders, from its iconic geysers and waterfalls to its abundant wildlife and hidden gems. With careful planning and a spirit of adventure, you're sure to create memories that will last a lifetime.

Family-Friendly Itinerary

Yellowstone National Park is a wonderland for families, offering a chance to connect with nature, witness incredible sights, and create lasting memories. This itinerary is designed with families in mind, focusing on accessible attractions, shorter hikes, and engaging activities that will appeal to all ages.

Day 1: Welcome to Yellowstone!

- Arrive at the South Entrance and head towards West Thumb Geyser Basin. The boardwalks are easy for little legs to navigate, and the colorful hot springs are a great introduction to Yellowstone's geothermal wonders.
- Enjoy a picnic lunch at Yellowstone Lake, taking in the breathtaking views and watching for wildlife along the shoreline.
- In the afternoon, head to Old Faithful and witness its iconic eruption. Kids will love the anticipation and excitement of this natural spectacle. Explore the Upper Geyser Basin and its many geysers and hot springs.
- Stay overnight at the Old Faithful Inn or Snow Lodge, both of which offer family-friendly accommodations and convenient access to nearby attractions.

Day 2: Waterfalls and Wildlife Adventures

- Start your day at the Grand Canyon of the Yellowstone, where you can witness the majestic Lower Falls from Artist Point. The viewpoint is easily accessible and offers stunning views of the canyon and the waterfall.
- Embark on a short, family-friendly hike on the South Rim Trail, enjoying the scenery and learning about the canyon's formation.
- In the afternoon, head to Lamar Valley, a prime spot for wildlife viewing. Keep your eyes peeled for bison, elk, and maybe even wolves! The valley's open landscape makes it easy to spot animals from the road.
- Stay overnight in the Mammoth Hot Springs area, enjoying the comfortable accommodations and the chance to explore the terraces in the evening.

Day 3: Learning and Exploration

- Visit the Mammoth Hot Springs Terraces and walk the boardwalks, marveling at the colorful travertine formations. Kids will love the unique shapes and textures of these natural wonders.
- Stop by the Albright Visitor Center and Museum, where interactive exhibits and displays will engage young minds and teach them about Yellowstone's history, geology, and wildlife.
- In the afternoon, head to Norris Geyser Basin, one of Yellowstone's most active geothermal areas. The short and easy walking paths make it accessible for families, and the colorful pools and geysers will capture everyone's attention.
- Spend the evening in Gardiner or Mammoth Hot Springs, enjoying a delicious meal at a family-friendly restaurant and reflecting on your Yellowstone adventures.

Additional Tips for a Family-Friendly Trip:

- Pack Snacks and Drinks: Keep everyone happy and hydrated with plenty of snacks and drinks, especially on longer drives and hikes.
- Plan for Breaks: Build in some downtime for relaxation and play, whether it's a picnic by a scenic lake or a visit to a playground.
- Engage with the Junior Ranger Program: Encourage your kids to participate in the Junior Ranger Program, where they can complete activities and earn a badge.

Adventure Seekers Itinerary

For those who crave adrenaline and seek out the untamed beauty of the wilderness, Yellowstone National Park offers a playground of adventure. This itinerary is designed for those who want to go beyond the typical tourist trail, challenge themselves physically, and experience the park's wild side.

Day 1: Arrival and Geothermal Exploration

- Arrive at the South Entrance and head towards West Thumb Geyser Basin. Instead of just strolling the boardwalks, embark on a kayaking adventure on Yellowstone Lake, paddling along the shoreline and exploring hidden coves.
- In the afternoon, hike the DeLacy Creek Trail, a moderate 5.8-mile loop that takes you through forests and meadows with stunning views of Shoshone Lake.
- As evening approaches, witness the eruption of Old Faithful, but instead of just watching from the boardwalk, hike to Observation Point for a panoramic perspective.
- Stay overnight in a backcountry campsite near Shoshone Lake, immersing yourself in the wilderness and enjoying the starry night sky.

Day 2: Conquering the Canyon and Wildlife Encounters

- Start your day with a challenging hike to the bottom of the Grand Canyon of the Yellowstone. Descend Uncle Tom's Trail, a steep staircase that leads to the brink of the Lower Falls, where you'll feel the mist on your face and witness the raw power of the waterfall.
- In the afternoon, embark on a whitewater rafting adventure on the Yellowstone River, navigating thrilling rapids and soaking in the canyon's grandeur from a unique perspective.
- As the day winds down, head to Lamar Valley and join a guided wolf-watching tour. With expert guides and spotting scopes, you'll increase your chances of encountering these elusive creatures in their natural habitat.
- Stay overnight in a rustic cabin near Lamar Valley, enjoying the peace and quiet of the wilderness.

Day 3: Summiting Peaks and Backcountry Exploration

- Challenge yourself with a strenuous hike to the summit of Mount Washburn, the highest point in the Washburn Range. The panoramic views from the top are well worth the effort.
- In the afternoon, embark on a multi-day backpacking trip into Yellowstone's backcountry. Obtain the necessary permits and plan your route carefully, choosing from a variety of trails that lead to remote lakes, alpine meadows, and hidden geothermal areas.
- Spend the next few days exploring the backcountry, setting up camp in designated areas, and immersing yourself in the solitude and beauty of Yellowstone's wilderness.

Day 6: Returning to Civilization and Saying Farewell

- As your backcountry adventure comes to an end, hike back to civilization and enjoy a hot shower and a hearty meal at a lodge or restaurant.
- Reflect on your adventurous journey through Yellowstone, the challenges you've overcome, and the unforgettable experiences you've had.
- Spend the evening relaxing and reminiscing about your time in the park, sharing stories and photos with fellow adventurers.

Day 7: Departure and Future Adventures

- Depart from Yellowstone, carrying with you a renewed sense of adventure and a deeper connection to the natural world.

- Plan your next adventure, inspired by the challenges and rewards of your Yellowstone experience.

This Adventure Seekers Itinerary offers a glimpse into the thrilling possibilities that await those who seek out the wild side of Yellowstone National Park. With careful planning, physical preparation, and a spirit of adventure, you can create an unforgettable experience that will push your limits and leave you with a profound appreciation for the park's untamed beauty.

CHAPTER 7: SEASONAL EVENTS AND FESTIVALS

Spring, Summer, Fall, and Winter Events

Yellowstone National Park is a year-round destination, with each season offering a unique tapestry of events and activities. Whether you're captivated by the vibrant colors of spring wildflowers, the thrill of summer wildlife watching, the golden hues of fall foliage, or the serene beauty of a winter wonderland, Yellowstone has something to offer every visitor throughout the year.

Spring (March-May)

As winter's grip loosens, Yellowstone awakens with a burst of new life. Wildflowers begin to paint the meadows with vibrant colors, and newborn animals take their first tentative steps. Spring is a time of renewal and a quieter time to visit the park, offering a more intimate experience of its natural wonders.

Join park rangers for guided wildflower walks, where you can learn about the diverse species that bloom in the park's meadows and forests. These walks typically take place in late May and early June when the flowers are at their peak.

Summer (June-August)

Summer is Yellowstone's peak season, with warm weather and long days inviting exploration and adventure. The park comes alive with visitors eager to witness its iconic geothermal features, hike its scenic trails, and encounter its abundant wildlife. Ranger-led programs are in full swing during the summer months, offering guided hikes, campfire talks, and wildlife-watching excursions. These programs provide a deeper understanding of the park's ecosystem, history, and geology.

Fall (September-November)

As summer fades, Yellowstone transforms into a haven of golden hues. The crowds begin to thin, and a sense of serenity settles over the park. Fall is a magical time to witness the changing colors of the leaves, the dramatic elk rut, and the wildlife preparing for winter. Hike through the park's forests and meadows, where the aspen and cottonwood trees put on a spectacular display of fall foliage. The cooler temperatures and crisp air make for invigorating hikes and scenic drives.

Winter (December-February)

Winter in Yellowstone is a truly unique experience. The park takes on a serene, snow-covered beauty, and the geothermal features create a mesmerizing contrast against the frosty landscape. While some roads may be closed to regular vehicles, winter opens up opportunities for snowshoeing, cross-country skiing, and snowmobiling. Wildlife watching in winter offers a different perspective, as animals like bison, elk, and wolves are often easier to spot against the snow. You might even catch a glimpse of a rare winter visitor, such as a snowy owl or a pine marten.

Throughout the Year

No matter when you choose to visit Yellowstone, you'll find a wealth of events and activities to enhance your experience. Check the park's official website or inquire at visitor centers for the latest information on ranger programs, guided tours, and special events happening during your visit. Whether you're seeking adventure, relaxation, or a deeper connection with nature, Yellowstone National Park offers a year-round tapestry of experiences to inspire and delight.

Annual Festivals In and Around the Park

Yellowstone National Park and its surrounding communities come alive throughout the year with a vibrant array of festivals and events. These celebrations offer a chance to immerse yourself in local culture, enjoy live music and entertainment, and experience the park's unique spirit. Here are some of the annual festivals you won't want to miss:

Yellowstone Winter Celebration (December)

As winter blankets Yellowstone in a pristine layer of snow, the Yellowstone Winter Celebration kicks off a season of festive cheer. This event takes place throughout December, with activities and festivities happening both within the park and in nearby towns. Inside the park, you can join ranger-led snowshoe hikes, learn about winter wildlife tracking, and even participate in photography workshops to capture the beauty of Yellowstone's winter landscapes. In the evenings, cozy up by the fire at one of the park's lodges and enjoy live music or storytelling.

The towns surrounding Yellowstone also join in the festivities, with holiday markets, craft fairs, and special events. You can find unique gifts, sample local cuisine, and enjoy the festive atmosphere.

Yellowstone National Park's Annual Fall Photography Contest (September-October)

For photography enthusiasts, the Annual Fall Photography Contest is a highlight of the Yellowstone calendar. As the park's foliage transforms into a breathtaking tapestry of golds, reds, and oranges, photographers of all skill levels are invited to capture the beauty and submit their best shots. The contest typically runs from September to October, coinciding with the peak of the fall colors. You can find details and submission guidelines on the park's official website. The winning photographs are often showcased in exhibits and publications, celebrating the artistry and capturing the essence of Yellowstone's autumn splendor.

The West Yellowstone Annual Snowmobile Expo (March)

West Yellowstone, Montana, known as the "Snowmobile Capital of the World," hosts an annual Snowmobile Expo in March, drawing enthusiasts from far and wide. This event is a celebration of all things snowmobiling, with opportunities to test out the latest models, gear up with the newest equipment, and connect with fellow riders. You can also join guided snowmobile tours into Yellowstone National Park, exploring the park's winter wonderland and experiencing its unique beauty from a different perspective. The expo also offers safety training and skills workshops, ensuring that riders of all levels can enjoy the sport responsibly.

Other Festivals and Events

The communities surrounding Yellowstone also host a variety of events throughout the year, from rodeos and music festivals to historical reenactments and art shows. Be sure to check local event calendars to see what's happening during your visit.

No matter when you choose to visit Yellowstone, you'll find a vibrant calendar of festivals and events that celebrate the park's unique spirit and offer a chance to connect with its rich culture and natural wonders.

Special Tours and Programs Offered in 2025

To enhance your visit to Yellowstone National Park, consider taking advantage of the special tours and programs offered throughout the year. These guided experiences provide unique opportunities to delve deeper into the park's wonders, learn from experts, and discover hidden gems you might otherwise miss.

Ranger-Led Tours and Programs

- **Wildlife-Watching Tours:** Join park rangers on guided tours through prime wildlife-watching areas like Lamar Valley and Hayden Valley. Learn about animal behavior, migration patterns, and conservation efforts while observing bison, wolves, elk, and more.
- **Geothermal and Geyser Tours:** Discover the science and history behind Yellowstone's geothermal features, such as Old Faithful and Grand Prismatic Spring. These tours offer insights into the formation, significance, and unique ecosystems of these natural wonders.
- **Historical Tours**: Explore the rich cultural history of Yellowstone, from the Native American tribes who first inhabited the area to the establishment of the park as the world's first national park. Learn about the development of Mammoth Hot Springs and the park's historic lodges and cabins.

Wildlife Safaris and Photography Tours

- **Lamar Valley Wolf-Watching Safaris**: Embark on an early morning safari through Lamar Valley, a prime location for spotting wolves and bison. Expert guides provide binoculars and spotting scopes for up-close views and share their knowledge about these fascinating creatures.
- **Photography Tours**: Capture the beauty of Yellowstone with specialized photography tours led by experienced photographers. Learn tips and techniques for photographing geysers, waterfalls, wildlife, and landscapes in various lighting and weather conditions.

Backcountry Hiking and Camping Tours

- **Guided Day Hikes:** Explore Yellowstone's backcountry trails with knowledgeable guides who share insights about the park's geology, history, and wildlife. Choose from a variety of trails, from moderate hikes to more challenging treks.
- **Multi-Day Backpacking Trips:** Immerse yourself in the wilderness with a multi-day backpacking adventure. Experienced guides assist with route planning, camping logistics, and provide interpretation of the surrounding environment.

Winter Tours

- **Snowcoach Tours**: When winter blankets Yellowstone in snow, explore the park's scenic wonders in a comfortable snowcoach. These guided tours provide access to areas closed to regular vehicles, allowing you to witness the park's winter beauty.
- **Snowmobile Tours:** For a more adventurous winter experience, join a guided snowmobile tour. These tours venture into the park's backcountry, offering opportunities for wildlife sightings and breathtaking views of snow-covered landscapes.

Volunteer and Stewardship Programs

- **Contribute to Conservation:** Give back to Yellowstone by participating in volunteer programs. Assist with trail maintenance, wildlife monitoring, or educational outreach. These programs offer a unique way to experience the park and make a positive impact.

Tips for Booking Tours and Programs

- Plan Ahead: Many tours and programs require reservations, especially during peak season. Book in advance to secure your spot.
- Check Availability: Tour schedules and availability vary throughout the year. Check the park's website or inquire at visitor centers for the latest information.
- Consider Your Interests: Choose tours and programs that align with your interests, whether it's wildlife watching, photography, history, or backcountry exploration.
- Pack Accordingly: Be prepared for the activities you'll be participating in, with appropriate clothing, footwear, and gear.

By taking advantage of the special tours and programs offered in Yellowstone, you can enhance your visit and create a more enriching and memorable experience. Whether you're seeking adventure, education, or a deeper connection with nature, these guided experiences provide a unique opportunity to discover the park's hidden treasures and gain a deeper appreciation for its wonders.

CHAPTER 8: STAYING SAFE IN YELLOWSTONE

Wildlife Safety

Yellowstone National Park is a truly wild place, and that's part of its magic. But with wild places come wild animals, and it's crucial to know how to safely interact with them during your visit. Remember, you're entering their home, and respecting their space ensures both your safety and the well-being of these incredible creatures.

Keeping Your Distance

The golden rule in Yellowstone is to maintain a safe distance from wildlife. While it's tempting to get closer for that perfect photo, remember that animals can be unpredictable, especially when they feel threatened or cornered. For your safety and theirs, follow these guidelines:

- **Bison:** Stay at least 25 yards away from these massive creatures. Despite their size, they can move surprisingly fast and can charge if they feel provoked.
- **Elk and Moose:** Keep a safe distance of 25 yards from elk and moose as well. They can be particularly protective during mating season.
- **Bears and Wolves:** These predators demand extra caution. Maintain at least 100 yards between yourself and bears or wolves. Never approach them, especially if they have cubs or pups.

- **Other Animals**: Even smaller creatures like marmots, bighorn sheep, and birds deserve their space. Avoid feeding or approaching them.

Don't Feed the Animals

It might seem harmless to offer a snack to a curious squirrel or bird, but feeding wildlife can have serious consequences. It disrupts their natural foraging behaviors, making them dependent on human food, which can lead to dangerous situations for both animals and people. Remember, feeding wildlife is not only unsafe but also illegal in Yellowstone.

Be Prepared for Animal Encounters

While most wildlife encounters in Yellowstone are peaceful, it's essential to be prepared. Here are some tips to keep in mind:

- **Carry Bear Spray:** If you're hiking or camping, carry bear spray and know how to use it. It's an effective deterrent if you encounter a bear too close for comfort.
- **Make Noise:** When hiking, especially in dense vegetation or near streams, make noise to alert animals to your presence. This helps prevent startling them and reduces the chance of a defensive reaction.
- **Stay Calm:** If you do encounter an animal, don't panic. Slowly back away and give the animal plenty of space to escape. Avoid making sudden movements or running, as this can trigger a chase response.

Respect Animal Habitats

Yellowstone is a sanctuary for its wildlife, so it's crucial to respect their natural habitats. Stay on designated trails and boardwalks, avoid approaching dens or nests, and never enter areas marked as closed or restricted. By respecting their space, we help ensure that Yellowstone's wildlife continues to thrive for generations to come.

How to Stay Safe While Hiking

Yellowstone's trails beckon with the promise of adventure and breathtaking scenery, but it's essential to prioritize safety during your hikes. By taking some precautions and being prepared, you can ensure a safe and enjoyable experience in the park's wild terrain.

Plan Ahead

Before you even set foot on a trail, take some time to plan your hike. Familiarize yourself with the trail's difficulty, length, and elevation gain. Check the park's website or visitor centers for any trail closures or advisories. Let someone know your hiking plans and expected return time.

Carry the Essentials

- Packing the right gear can make all the difference in ensuring a safe and comfortable hike. Here are some essentials to bring:
- Water: Stay hydrated by carrying plenty of water, especially on longer hikes. Consider a water filter or purification tablets if you plan to refill from natural sources.
- Snacks: Pack energy-boosting snacks like trail mix, granola bars, or fruit to keep you fueled throughout your hike.

- Navigation: Bring a map, compass, or GPS device, and familiarize yourself with the trail's route. Don't rely solely on your phone, as cell service can be spotty in some areas.
- Sun Protection: Protect yourself from the sun with sunscreen, sunglasses, and a hat.
- First Aid Kit: A basic first aid kit can come in handy for minor injuries.
- Extra Layers: Be prepared for changing weather conditions with extra layers of clothing, including a rain jacket and a warm fleece or sweater.

Watch for Wildlife

Yellowstone is home to a variety of wildlife, including bears, bison, and elk. While encounters can be thrilling, it's important to be cautious and respectful.

- Make Noise: When hiking, make noise to alert animals to your presence. Talk, sing, or clap your hands periodically, especially in areas with dense vegetation.
- Carry Bear Spray: If you're hiking in bear country, carry bear spray and know how to use it.
- Stay Alert: Be aware of your surroundings and watch for signs of wildlife, such as tracks, scat, or sounds.
- Keep Your Distance: If you see an animal, maintain a safe distance and never approach or feed it. Use binoculars or a telephoto lens to get a closer look.

Know the Weather

Yellowstone's weather can be unpredictable, with sudden changes in temperature and conditions. Be prepared for rain, snow, or thunderstorms, even during the summer months. Check the forecast before you go and be prepared to adjust your plans if necessary.

Stay on Marked Trails

For your safety and the preservation of the park's fragile ecosystem, always stay on marked trails. Wandering off-trail can lead to disorientation, injuries, and damage to the environment. By following these safety tips and using common sense, you can enjoy a safe and rewarding hiking experience in Yellowstone National Park. Remember, you're a guest in this wild and wonderful place, so treat it with respect and prioritize your safety at all times.

CHAPTER 9: DAY TRIPS AND NEARBY ATTRACTIONS

Exploring Grand Teton National Park

Just south of Yellowstone lies another gem of the American West: Grand Teton National Park. With its towering, jagged peaks, pristine lakes, and abundant wildlife, Grand Teton offers a stunning contrast to the geothermal wonders of Yellowstone and is a must-visit for those seeking more adventure. Imagine standing before the majestic Teton Range, its peaks reflecting in the crystal-clear waters of Jenny Lake. Hike through wildflower meadows, witness moose grazing in the marshes, and keep your eyes peeled for soaring bald eagles. Grand Teton is a paradise for outdoor enthusiasts and nature lovers alike.

Getting There

From Yellowstone's South Entrance, it's a short and scenic drive to Grand Teton National Park. Follow the John D. Rockefeller, Jr. Memorial Parkway, a 24-mile scenic roadway that connects the two parks. The drive itself is an experience, with the Teton Range rising dramatically in the distance.

What to Do

- **Jenny Lake:** Take a scenic boat ride across Jenny Lake, or hike the Jenny Lake Loop Trail for breathtaking views of the Tetons and the surrounding scenery.

- **Scenic Drives:** Explore the park's scenic drives, such as Teton Park Road and Moose-Wilson Road, stopping at overlooks like Snake River Overlook for iconic photo opportunities.
- **Hiking**: Choose from a variety of hiking trails, ranging from easy lakeside strolls to challenging mountain climbs. Cascade Canyon and Paintbrush Canyon offer rewarding hikes with stunning views.
- **Wildlife Watching:** Grand Teton is home to a diverse array of wildlife. Look for bison, elk, moose, pronghorn, and even bears in the park's meadows and forests.
- **Photography:** With its majestic mountains, pristine lakes, and abundant wildlife, Grand Teton is a photographer's dream. Capture the beauty of the Teton Range, the serenity of Jenny Lake, and the wildlife encounters that make this park so special.

Where to Stay

- **In-Park Lodging:** Grand Teton offers a variety of lodging options within the park, from historic lodges to cozy cabins. Jenny Lake Lodge and Jackson Lake Lodge are popular choices.
- **Jackson Hole:** The town of Jackson, located just outside the park's southern boundary, offers a wide range of accommodations, from budget-friendly motels to luxurious resorts.

Additional Tips

- Plan Your Visit: Grand Teton can be crowded, especially during the summer months. Make reservations for lodging and activities in advance.
- Respect Wildlife: Maintain a safe distance from animals and never approach or feed them.
- Pack for All Weather: Be prepared for sudden changes in weather, as mountain conditions can be unpredictable.
- Leave No Trace: Pack out all trash and dispose of it properly to help preserve the park's pristine environment.

Grand Teton National Park is a must-visit destination for those seeking adventure and natural beauty. With its towering peaks, pristine lakes, and abundant wildlife, it offers a unique and unforgettable experience that complements a visit to Yellowstone National Park.

Scenic Towns to Visit Near Yellowstone

While Yellowstone National Park is a destination in itself, the areas surrounding the park offer charming towns and unique experiences that can enhance your trip. These towns provide a change of pace from the wilderness, with opportunities to explore local culture, enjoy delicious food, and discover hidden gems.

Jackson, Wyoming

Nestled at the base of the Teton Mountain Range, Jackson is a picturesque town with a vibrant atmosphere. Stroll through the historic town square, framed by elk antler arches, and browse the local shops and art galleries. Visit the National Museum of Wildlife Art to admire stunning works inspired by the region's natural beauty.

West Yellowstone, Montana

Located just outside the West Entrance of Yellowstone, West Yellowstone is a bustling town that caters to park visitors. Enjoy a delicious meal at the Geyser Grill, learn about the park's history at the Yellowstone Historic Center, or take a scenic drive to Hebgen Lake for breathtaking views.

Gardiner, Montana

As the North Entrance to Yellowstone, Gardiner offers a blend of small-town charm and easy access to the park's wonders. Take a dip in the Boiling River, a natural hot spring where you can soak while enjoying views of the Yellowstone River. Don't miss the iconic Roosevelt Arch, a historic landmark that marks the gateway to the park.

Cody, Wyoming

Venture east to Cody, a town steeped in Wild West history and named after its founder, Buffalo Bill Cody. Immerse yourself in the history of the American West at the Buffalo Bill Center of the West, a world-class museum complex. For a taste of cowboy culture, attend the Cody Nite Rodeo, a thrilling spectacle of skill and daring.

Bozeman, Montana

Located about 90 miles north of Yellowstone, Bozeman is a vibrant college town with a thriving arts and culture scene. Explore the Museum of the Rockies, home to an impressive collection of dinosaur fossils, or stroll through downtown Bozeman, with its unique shops, local cafes, and art galleries.

These are just a few of the charming towns that await you near Yellowstone National Park. Each offers its own unique character and attractions, providing a delightful complement to your wilderness adventures.

Visiting the Montana and Wyoming Surroundings

While Yellowstone National Park is a captivating destination, don't miss the opportunity to explore the diverse landscapes and charming towns of Montana and Wyoming that lie just beyond the park's borders. These surrounding areas offer a chance to delve deeper into the region's history, culture, and natural beauty, adding another dimension to your Yellowstone adventure.

Jackson Hole, Wyoming

Just south of Grand Teton National Park, Jackson Hole is a vibrant valley surrounded by majestic mountains. The town of Jackson, with its historic town square and iconic elk antler arches, exudes a charming Western atmosphere. Explore the shops and art galleries, or visit the National Museum of Wildlife Art to admire stunning depictions of the region's fauna. For outdoor enthusiasts, Jackson Hole offers opportunities for hiking, wildlife watching, and scenic drives.

Cody, Wyoming

To the east of Yellowstone lies Cody, a town steeped in Wild West history and named after its founder, Buffalo Bill Cody. Immerse yourself in the history of the American West at the Buffalo Bill Center of the West, a renowned museum complex.

Montana's Gateway Towns

Montana offers several charming towns that serve as gateways to Yellowstone National Park.

- **Gardiner:** Located at the park's North Entrance, Gardiner boasts a historic district and the iconic Roosevelt Arch. Explore the shops and restaurants, or take a dip in the Boiling River, a natural hot spring where the Gardiner River's cold water mixes with the hot spring water.
- **West Yellowstone:** Just outside the West Entrance, West Yellowstone is a popular hub for visitors. Discover the Grizzly & Wolf Discovery Center, learn about the park's history at the Yellowstone Historic Center, or enjoy a delicious meal at one of the town's many restaurants.
- **Bozeman:** About 90 miles north of Yellowstone, Bozeman is a vibrant college town with a thriving arts and culture scene. Explore the Museum of the Rockies, home to an impressive collection of dinosaur fossils, or hike the "M" Trail for panoramic views of the Gallatin Valley.

Beyond the Towns

Venture further into Montana and Wyoming to discover more scenic wonders.

- **Paradise Valley:** This picturesque valley, located south of Livingston, Montana, offers stunning mountain views, dude ranches, and opportunities for fly fishing and horseback riding.
- **Red Lodge, Montana:** Nestled in the Beartooth Mountains, Red Lodge is a charming town with a rich mining history. Take a scenic drive on the Beartooth Highway, hike to scenic overlooks, or explore the Beartooth Mountains.
- **The Wind River Range, Wyoming:** For those seeking a true wilderness experience, the Wind River Range offers rugged mountains, pristine lakes, and challenging hiking trails.

By venturing beyond Yellowstone's boundaries, you can add another layer of depth and adventure to your trip. These surrounding towns and landscapes offer a chance to connect with the region's history, culture, and natural beauty, creating a more enriching and memorable experience.

CHAPTER 10: PRACTICAL TRAVEL INFORMATION

Entrance Fees and Passes

Planning your trip to Yellowstone National Park involves understanding the park's entrance fees and the various passes available. These fees and passes help support the park's infrastructure, services, and ongoing conservation efforts.

Entrance Fees

Yellowstone National Park charges an entrance fee for all visitors, with varying rates depending on your mode of entry. Here's a breakdown of the fees:

- Private Vehicle: $35 (admits private, non-commercial vehicles with capacity for 15 or fewer passengers)
- Motorcycle: $30
- Individual (on foot, bicycle, or ski): $20

These entrance fees are valid for 7 days, allowing you to enter and exit the park multiple times during that period.

Annual and Multi-Visit Passes

If you plan to visit Yellowstone more than once within a year or explore other national parks, consider purchasing a pass to save money.

Yellowstone Annual Pass: $70

This pass provides unlimited entry to Yellowstone National Park for 12 months from the date of purchase. It's ideal for frequent visitors or those who plan to explore the park extensively.

America the Beautiful - The National Parks and Federal Recreational Lands Pass: $80

This pass grants access to over 2,000 federal recreation sites across the United States, including all national parks. It's a great option for those planning to visit multiple parks or federal lands within a year.

Senior Pass (America the Beautiful): $20 (annual) or $80 (lifetime)

U.S. citizens or permanent residents aged 62 or older can purchase this pass at a discounted rate. It offers the same benefits as the America the Beautiful Pass, providing access to national parks and federal recreational lands.

Access Pass: Free

U.S. citizens or permanent residents with permanent disabilities can obtain this pass for free access to national parks and federal lands.

Where to Buy Passes

You can purchase entrance passes at any of Yellowstone's entrance stations, visitor centers, or online through the USGS store.

Other Fee Information

- Camping Fees: If you plan to camp within Yellowstone, there are additional fees for campsites, which vary depending on the location and amenities.
- Tour Fees: Guided tours, such as snowmobile rentals, wildlife safaris, and ranger-led programs, may have separate fees.

By understanding the entrance fees and pass options, you can make the most of your visit to Yellowstone National Park while supporting its preservation and conservation efforts.

Park Hours and Seasonal Closures (2025)

Yellowstone National Park is a vast and dynamic wilderness, and its accessibility can vary throughout the year due to weather conditions and seasonal changes. To make the most of your visit, it's essential to understand the park's hours of operation and any potential closures that may affect your travel plans.

Park Hours

Yellowstone is open 24 hours a day, 365 days a year. However, specific facilities and services within the park operate on varying schedules.

- **Visitor Centers:** The park's visitor centers offer exhibits, educational programs, and helpful staff to assist with trip planning. Each visitor center has its own operating hours, which may change depending on the season. Be sure to check the park's website or inquire at a visitor center for the most up-to-date information.
- **Roads:** Most of Yellowstone's roads are open year-round, but some may close temporarily due to snow, ice, or road construction. The park's website provides real-time updates on road conditions and closures.

- **Lodging and Campgrounds:** Yellowstone offers a variety of lodging options within the park, including historic hotels, cabins, and campgrounds. These facilities typically operate on a seasonal basis, with some closing during the winter months. Check the availability and operating dates for your desired lodging option when planning your trip.

Seasonal Closures

- **Winter Closures:** During the winter months, typically from November to April, some park roads may be closed to regular vehicles due to snow and ice. However, you can still access certain areas of the park through guided snowmobile or snowcoach tours.
- **Spring and Fall Closures:** Some roads and facilities may also have limited access or closures during the shoulder seasons of spring and fall due to weather conditions or maintenance.

Best Times to Visit

- **Summer (June-September):** This is peak season in Yellowstone, with all roads and facilities typically open. Expect larger crowds and warmer weather, ideal for hiking, wildlife watching, and exploring the park's geothermal features.
- **Fall (September-November):** As the crowds begin to disperse, fall offers a quieter experience with stunning foliage and opportunities for wildlife viewing, such as the elk rut. Some services may start to close in mid-September as the weather cools.
- **Winter (December-March):** For a unique and serene experience, consider visiting Yellowstone in winter. While some roads may be closed, you can enjoy winter activities like snowshoeing, cross-country skiing, and snowmobiling.
- **Spring (April-June):** Spring brings new life to Yellowstone, with wildflowers blooming and newborn animals appearing. It's a quieter time to visit, but be prepared for unpredictable weather and potential road closures.

Staying Informed

To ensure a smooth and enjoyable visit, stay informed about park hours, seasonal closures, and any potential alerts or advisories. Check the park's official website or inquire at visitor centers for the most up-to-date information. By planning accordingly, you can make the most of your time in Yellowstone National Park and experience its wonders in any season.

Contact Information for Services and Emergencies

Yellowstone National Park is a vast and wild place, and while we all hope for a smooth and carefree visit, it's essential to be prepared for unexpected situations. Whether you need information about park services, encounter an emergency, or simply want to inquire about road conditions, knowing the right contact information can make all the difference.

General Information and Park Services

- **Park Headquarters:** For general inquiries, park updates, or assistance with planning your visit, you can contact Yellowstone National Park Headquarters at (307) 344-7381 or visit their website at Yellowstone National Park Official Website. Google Search for "Yellowstone National Park contact information"
- **Visitor Centers:** Each of the park's visitor centers also has its own contact number, which you can find on the park's website or by inquiring at the visitor center directly.

Emergency Contacts

- **Emergencies:** In case of any emergency within the park, dial 911. This will connect you with park rangers who can provide immediate assistance.

- **Non-Emergencies:** For non-emergency assistance, you can contact Yellowstone dispatch at (307) 344-7381.
- **Medical Emergencies:** For medical emergencies, contact the Yellowstone Clinic at (307) 344-7965. The clinic is open seasonally and provides care for minor injuries and health issues.
- **Wildlife Encounters:** If you encounter wildlife that is behaving aggressively or posing a danger, contact Yellowstone Rangers at (307) 344-7381 or the Wildlife Safety Hotline at (307) 344-4007.

Medical and Fire Services Outside the Park

- **Hospitals:** For serious medical emergencies or those requiring hospitalization, the nearest emergency room is at St. John's Health in Jackson, Wyoming, at (307) 733-3636.
- **Fire Emergencies:** For fire-related emergencies within the park, contact the Yellowstone Fire Department at (307) 344-7381. For emergencies outside the park, dial 911.

Road Conditions and Travel Alerts

- **Road Status:** For updated information on road conditions, closures, and travel alerts, call the Yellowstone Road Condition Hotline at (307) 344-2111 or visit the park's website.

Lost and Found

- **Lost Items:** If you lose an item within the park, contact Yellowstone dispatch at (307) 344-7381 to report it.

Remember, being prepared and knowing the right contact information can help ensure a safe and enjoyable visit to Yellowstone National Park. Don't hesitate to reach out to park staff or emergency services if needed.

Accessibility and Special Needs

Yellowstone National Park is committed to providing an inclusive and enjoyable experience for all visitors, regardless of their abilities. The park offers a variety of services and facilities to ensure accessibility for those with disabilities, allowing everyone to experience the wonders of Yellowstone.

Accessible Roads, Trails, and Viewpoints

Many of the park's main roads are paved and suitable for wheelchairs and other mobility devices. Accessible parking spaces are available at major attractions and visitor centers. Several trails are also wheelchair-friendly, including boardwalks around geysers and accessible viewing areas for wildlife watching.

Wheelchair-Accessible Lodging and Services

Yellowstone offers wheelchair-accessible rooms in several of its lodges, equipped with wider doors, ramps, and other features for convenience. Wheelchair rentals are available at no cost at various locations, and many restrooms at visitor centers and major attractions are wheelchair accessible.

Adaptive Programs and Tours

The park provides adaptive programs and tours for visitors with visual, auditory, and mobility impairments. Sign language interpreters are available for some ranger-led programs, and specialized tours cater to those using wheelchairs or scooters. Audio tours are also available for visitors with visual impairments.

Services for Hearing-Impaired Visitors

Yellowstone offers services for deaf or hard-of-hearing visitors, including text-based services at visitor centers and ranger-led programs with closed captioning or visual aids.

Accessibility Resources and Contacts

The park's official website provides a comprehensive Accessibility Guide with detailed information about available services, accommodations, and accessible amenities. You can also contact Yellowstone National Park at (307) 344-7381 for accessibility-related questions.

Yellowstone National Park is dedicated to ensuring that all visitors have an opportunity to experience its wonders. With its accessible facilities, adaptive programs, and commitment to inclusivity, Yellowstone welcomes everyone to explore its breathtaking landscapes and create lasting memories.

CONCLUSION

As we conclude our journey through the pages of this Yellowstone National Park Travel Guide, I hope you feel inspired and well-equipped to embark on your own adventure. Remember those breathtaking images we painted together—the raw power of Old Faithful, the kaleidoscope of colors at Grand Prismatic Spring, the thundering waterfalls of the Grand Canyon of the Yellowstone, and the serene beauty of Yellowstone Lake.

More than just a park, Yellowstone is a sanctuary—a place where the earth reveals its ancient history, where wildlife roams freely, and where you can disconnect from the everyday and reconnect with the wonders of the natural world.

Whether you're seeking adventure on challenging hikes, tranquility amidst serene landscapes, or simply a deeper connection with nature, Yellowstone has something for everyone. As you wander through its vast wilderness, remember you're walking in the footsteps of explorers, adventurers, and those who have sought solace and inspiration in its beauty. Take the memories you've created within these pages and weave them into your own Yellowstone story. Share your experiences, protect this precious land, and return often to discover new facets of its ever-changing beauty.

Until next time, may the spirit of Yellowstone stay with you, reminding you of the power of nature, the importance of preservation, and the joy of exploration. Safe travels, and may your adventures be filled with wonder.

Bonus: Your Ultimate Packing List & Guide to Identifying Local Flora and Fauna

As you prepare for your Yellowstone adventure, packing the right gear can make all the difference in your experience. This comprehensive packing list ensures you're ready for anything, from sudden weather changes to unexpected wildlife encounters. Plus, a handy guide to identifying Yellowstone's diverse flora and fauna will deepen your connection to the park's natural wonders.

Packing List for All Seasons

Yellowstone's weather is notoriously unpredictable, so it's best to be prepared for anything. Layering is key, and packing versatile clothing items will allow you to adapt to changing conditions.

Spring (April-June)

- Waterproof jacket and pants
- Warm layers (sweaters, fleece)
- Hiking boots with good traction
- Moisture-wicking socks

- Gloves and a warm hat
- Daypack
- Water bottle or hydration reservoir
- First-aid kit
- Sunscreen and sunglasses
- Insect repellent
- Binoculars
- Camera

Summer (July-September)

- Lightweight, moisture-wicking clothing
- Hiking shorts and pants
- Long-sleeved shirts for sun protection
- Wide-brimmed hat and sunglasses
- Sturdy hiking boots
- Daypack
- Water bottle or hydration reservoir
- High-SPF sunscreen and lip balm
- Insect repellent
- Camera with extra batteries and memory cards
- Headlamp or flashlight

Fall (October-November)

- Warm layers (sweaters, fleece, insulated jacket)
- Waterproof and windproof outer layers
- Hiking boots with good ankle support
- Warm socks, gloves, and a hat
- Daypack
- Water bottle or hydration reservoir
- First-aid kit
- Headlamp or flashlight
- Binoculars

Winter (December-March)

- Heavy-duty insulated jacket and pants
- Waterproof and insulated boots
- Thermal underwear and layers
- Warm hat, gloves, and neck gaiter
- Daypack or backpack

- Water bottle or thermos
- High-calorie snacks
- Navigation tools (map, compass, GPS)
- First-aid kit
- Headlamp or flashlight

Guide to Identifying Local Flora and Fauna

Yellowstone is home to a rich diversity of plants and animals. Here are a few common ones you might encounter:

Flora

- Lodgepole Pine: Tall, slender trees with reddish-brown bark.
- Whitebark Pine: Hardy, high-elevation pines with white bark.
- Douglas Fir: Tall evergreen trees with a distinctive cone.
- Aspen: Deciduous trees known for their white bark and golden fall foliage.
- Indian Paintbrush: Bright red or orange wildflowers.
- Yellow Monkeyflower: Yellow, trumpet-shaped wildflowers.

Fauna

- Bison: Large, shaggy mammals that roam in herds.
- Elk: The largest member of the deer family, with males sporting impressive antlers.
- Moose: The largest member of the deer family, with a distinctive hump on their shoulders.
- Wolves: Elusive predators that often travel in packs.
- Grizzly Bears: Large, powerful bears with a distinctive hump on their shoulders.
- Black Bears: Smaller than grizzlies, with a variety of coat colors.
- Pronghorn: The fastest land mammal in North America.
- Bighorn Sheep: Majestic animals with large, curled horns.

This packing list and identification guide will help you prepare for your Yellowstone adventure and enhance your appreciation for the park's natural wonders. Remember to pack for all types of weather, respect wildlife, and leave no trace of your visit.

MY TRAVEL PLAN

TRAVEL ITINERARY

Date: ----------------

S S M T W T F

	6 AM	
	7 AM	
	8 AM	
	9 AM	
	10 AM	
	11 AM	
	12 PM	
	1 PM	
	2 PM	
	3 PM	
	4 PM	
	5 PM	
	6 PM	
	7 PM	
	8 PM	

NOTE:

MY PACKING LIST

TRAVEL
ITINERARY

Date: _____

S S M T W T F

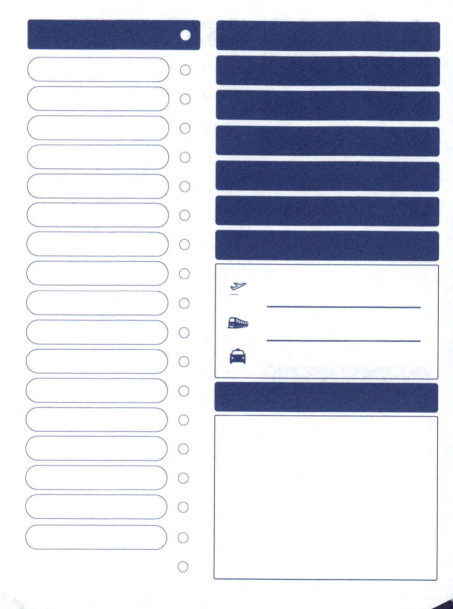

PLACES TO VISIT

TRAVEL ITINERARY

Date: _____

S S M T W T F

	☆☆☆☆☆☆☆☆☆☆
	☆☆☆☆☆☆☆☆☆☆
	☆☆☆☆☆☆☆☆☆☆
	☆☆☆☆☆☆☆☆☆☆
	☆☆☆☆☆☆☆☆☆☆
	☆☆☆☆☆☆☆☆☆☆
	☆☆☆☆☆☆☆☆☆☆
	☆☆☆☆☆☆☆☆☆☆
	☆☆☆☆☆☆☆☆☆☆
	☆☆☆☆☆☆☆☆☆☆
	☆☆☆☆☆☆☆☆☆☆
	☆☆☆☆☆☆☆☆☆☆
	☆☆☆☆☆☆☆☆☆☆
	☆☆☆☆☆☆☆☆☆☆

TRAVEL JOURNAL

TRAVEL REVIEW

TRAVEL JOURNAL

TRAVEL REVIEW

Date: ------------------

S S M T W T F

TRAVEL JOURNAL
TRAVEL REVIEW

TRAVEL JOURNAL

TRAVEL REVIEW

Date: _____

S S M T W T F

TRAVEL JOURNAL

TRAVEL REVIEW

TRAVEL JOURNAL

TRAVEL REVIEW

Date: _____

S S M T W T F

THANK YOU

FOR VISITING YELLOWSTONE NATIONAL PARK